THE BEST OF SECRET

RESTAURANT

★ RECIPES ★

pil

Publications International, Ltd.

Pictured on the front cover *(clockwise from top left):* Double Decker Tacos
(page 134), Creamy Tomato Soup *(page 56),* Steakhouse Chopped Salad
(page 68), Raspberry White Chocolate Cheesecake *(page 160),* Bangkok
Peanut Noodles *(page 126)* and Chicken Parmesan Sliders *(page 32).*

Pictured on the back cover *(left to right):* Chicken Lettuce Wraps *(page 40),*
Chicken Bowtie Party *(page 132)* and Berry Crumble Bars *(page 176).*

Let's get social!
 @Publications_International
 @PublicationsInternational
www.pilbooks.com

TABLE OF CONTENTS

BREAKFAST and BRUNCH

FRITTATA RUSTICA

MAKES 2 SERVINGS

4 ounces cremini mushrooms, stems trimmed, cut into thirds

1 tablespoon olive oil, divided

½ teaspoon plus ⅛ teaspoon salt, divided

½ cup chopped onion

1 cup packed chopped stemmed lacinato kale

½ cup halved grape tomatoes

4 eggs

½ teaspoon Italian seasoning

Black pepper

⅓ cup shredded mozzarella cheese

1 tablespoon shredded Parmesan cheese

Chopped fresh parsley (optional)

1 Preheat oven to 400°F. Spread mushrooms on small baking sheet; drizzle with 1 teaspoon oil and sprinkle with ⅛ teaspoon salt. Roast 15 to 20 minutes or until well browned and tender.

2 Heat remaining 2 teaspoons oil in small nonstick skillet over medium heat. Add onion; cook and stir 5 minutes or until soft. Add kale and ¼ teaspoon salt; cook and stir 10 minutes or until kale is tender. Add tomatoes; cook and stir 3 minutes or until tomatoes are soft. Stir in mushrooms.

3 Preheat broiler. Whisk eggs, remaining ¼ teaspoon salt, Italian seasoning and pepper in small bowl until well blended.

4 Pour egg mixture over vegetables in skillet; stir gently to mix. Cook about 3 minutes or until eggs are set around edge, lifting edge to allow uncooked portion to flow underneath. Sprinkle with mozzarella and Parmesan. Broil 3 minutes or until eggs are set and cheese is browned. Garnish with parsley.

RICH AND GOOEY CINNAMON BUNS

MAKES 12 BUNS

DOUGH

- 1 package (¼ ounce) active dry yeast
- 1 cup warm milk (110°F)
- 2 eggs, beaten
- ½ cup granulated sugar
- ¼ cup (½ stick) butter, softened
- 1 teaspoon salt
- 4 to 4¼ cups all-purpose flour

FILLING

- 1 cup packed brown sugar
- 3 tablespoons ground cinnamon
- Pinch salt
- 6 tablespoons (¾ stick) butter, softened

ICING

- 1½ cups powdered sugar
- 3 ounces cream cheese, softened
- ¼ cup (½ stick) butter, softened
- ½ teaspoon vanilla
- ⅛ teaspoon salt

1 Dissolve yeast in warm milk in large bowl of electric stand mixer. Add eggs, granulated sugar, ¼ cup butter and 1 teaspoon salt; beat at medium speed until well blended. Add 4 cups flour; beat at low speed until dough begins to come together. Knead dough with dough hook at low speed about 5 minutes or until dough is smooth, elastic and slightly sticky. Add additional flour, 1 tablespoon at a time, if necessary to prevent sticking.

2 Shape dough into a ball. Place in large greased bowl; turn to grease top. Cover and let rise in warm place about 1 hour or until doubled in size. Meanwhile, for filling, combine brown sugar, cinnamon and pinch of salt in small bowl; mix well.

3 Spray 13×9-inch baking pan with nonstick cooking spray. Roll out dough into 18×14-inch rectangle on floured surface. Spread 6 tablespoons butter evenly over dough; top with cinnamon-sugar mixture. Beginning with long side, roll up dough tightly jelly-roll style; pinch seam to seal. Cut log crosswise into 12 slices; place slices cut sides up in prepared pan. Cover and let rise in warm place about 30 minutes or until almost doubled in size. Preheat oven to 350°F.

4 Bake 20 to 25 minutes or until golden brown. Meanwhile, for icing, combine powdered sugar, cream cheese, ¼ cup butter, vanilla and ⅛ teaspoon salt in medium bowl; beat with electric mixer at medium speed 2 minutes or until smooth and creamy. Spread icing generously over warm cinnamon buns.

STUFFED HASH BROWNS

MAKES 1 TO 2 SERVINGS

1½ cups shredded potatoes*
2 tablespoons finely chopped onion
¼ plus ⅛ teaspoon salt, divided
⅛ teaspoon black pepper
2 tablespoons butter, divided
1 tablespoon vegetable oil

½ cup diced ham (¼-inch pieces)
3 eggs
2 tablespoons milk
2 slices American cheese

Use refrigerated shredded hash brown potatoes or shredded peeled russet potatoes, squeezed dry.

1 Preheat oven to 250°F. Place wire rack over baking sheet. Combine potatoes, onion, ¼ teaspoon salt and pepper in medium bowl; mix well.

2 Heat 1 tablespoon butter and oil in small (6- to 8-inch) nonstick skillet over medium heat. Add potato mixture; spread to cover bottom of skillet evenly, pressing down gently with spatula to flatten. Cook about 10 minutes or until bottom and edges are golden brown. Cover skillet with large inverted plate; carefully flip hash browns onto plate. Slide hash browns back into skillet, cooked side up. Cook 10 minutes or until golden brown. Slide hash browns onto prepared wire rack; place in oven to keep warm while preparing ham and eggs.

3 Melt 1 teaspoon butter in same skillet over medium-high heat. Add ham; cook and stir 2 to 3 minutes or until lightly browned. Remove to plate.

4 Whisk eggs, milk and remaining ⅛ teaspoon salt in small bowl until well blended. Melt remaining 2 teaspoons butter in same skillet over medium-high heat. Add egg mixture; cook about 3 minutes or just until eggs are cooked through, stirring to form large, fluffy curds. Place cheese slices on top of eggs; remove from heat and cover skillet to melt cheese.

5 Cut hash browns in half. Place one half on serving plate; sprinkle with ham. Top with eggs and remaining half of hash browns.

TIP

Refrigerated shredded potatoes are very wet when first removed from the package. For the best results, dry them well with paper towels before cooking.

SWEET POTATO PANCAKES
MAKES 5 SERVINGS (10 LARGE PANCAKES)

PANCAKES
- 2 medium sweet potatoes
- 2½ cups all-purpose flour
- 1 teaspoon baking powder
- 1 teaspoon baking soda
- ½ teaspoon salt
- ½ teaspoon ground cinnamon
- ¼ teaspoon ground ginger
- 2¾ cups buttermilk
- 2 eggs
- 2 tablespoons packed brown sugar
- 2 tablespoons butter, melted and cooled, plus additional for pan

GINGER BUTTER
- ¼ cup (½ stick) butter, softened
- 1 tablespoon packed brown sugar
- 1 teaspoon grated fresh ginger
- Pinch salt
- Prepared caramel sauce or maple syrup
- ¾ cup chopped glazed pecans*

Glazed or candied pecans may be found in the produce section of the supermarket along with other salad convenience items, or they may be found in the snack aisle.

1 Preheat oven to 375°F. Scrub sweet potatoes; bake 55 minutes or until soft. Cool slightly; peel and mash. Measure out 1⅓ cups for pancake batter.

2 Combine flour, baking powder, baking soda, salt, cinnamon and ground ginger in medium bowl; mix well. Whisk buttermilk, eggs and 2 tablespoons brown sugar in large bowl until well blended. Stir in 2 tablespoons butter. Add sweet potatoes; whisk until well blended. Add flour mixture; stir just until dry ingredients are moistened and no streaks of flour remain. Do not overmix; batter will be lumpy. Let stand 10 minutes.

3 Heat griddle or large skillet* over medium heat; brush with butter to coat. For each pancake, pour ½ cup of batter onto griddle, spreading into 5- to 6-inch circle. Cook about 4 minutes or until bottom is golden brown and small bubbles appear on surface. Turn pancake; cook about 3 minutes or until golden brown. Add additional butter to griddle as needed.

4 For ginger butter, beat ¼ cup softened butter, 1 tablespoon brown sugar, fresh ginger and pinch of salt in small bowl until well blended. If using caramel sauce, microwave according to package directions. Stir in water, 1 teaspoon at a time, to thin to desired pouring consistency. Serve pancakes warm topped with ginger butter, caramel sauce and glazed pecans.

Since pancakes are large, a skillet may not hold more than one pancake at a time. Keep pancakes warm in a 250°F oven on a wire rack set over a baking sheet.

PUMPKIN BREAD
MAKES 2 LOAVES

2¼ cups all-purpose flour

1 tablespoon pumpkin pie spice

1 teaspoon baking powder

1 teaspoon baking soda

¾ teaspoon salt

3 eggs

1 can (15 ounces) pure pumpkin

1 cup granulated sugar

1 cup packed brown sugar

⅔ cup vegetable oil

1 teaspoon vanilla

¼ cup roasted salted pumpkin seeds, coarsely chopped or crushed

1 Preheat oven to 350°F. Spray two 8×4-inch loaf pans with nonstick cooking spray.

2 Combine flour, pumpkin pie spice, baking powder, baking soda and salt in medium bowl; mix well.

3 Beat eggs in large bowl. Add pumpkin, granulated sugar, brown sugar, oil and vanilla; whisk until well blended. Add flour mixture; stir just until dry ingredients are moistened. Divide batter between prepared pans; smooth top. Sprinkle with pumpkin seeds; pat seeds gently into batter to adhere.

4 Bake about 50 minutes or until toothpick inserted into centers comes out mostly clean with just a few moist crumbs. Cool in pans 10 minutes; remove to wire racks to cool completely.

NOTE

The recipe can be made in one 9×5-inch loaf pan instead of two 8×4-inch pans. Bake about 1 hour 20 minutes or until toothpick inserted into center comes out with just a few moist crumbs. Check bread after 50 minutes; cover loosely with foil if top is browning too quickly.

SPINACH ARTICHOKE EGG SOUFFLÉS

MAKES 8 SERVINGS

- 1 package (about 17 ounces) frozen puff pastry (2 sheets), thawed
- 1 teaspoon olive oil
- ¼ cup chopped onion
- 1 clove garlic, minced
- ¼ cup finely chopped roasted red pepper (1 pepper)
- ¼ cup finely chopped canned artichoke hearts (about 2 medium)
- ¼ cup frozen chopped spinach, thawed and squeezed dry
- 3 eggs, separated
- ½ (8-ounce) package cream cheese, softened
- ½ teaspoon salt
- ⅛ teaspoon black pepper
- 4 tablespoons grated Romano cheese, divided

1 Preheat oven to 400°F. Spray eight 4-inch or 1-cup ramekins or jumbo (3½-inch) muffin pan cups with nonstick cooking spray. Unfold puff pastry; cut each sheet into quarters. Gently press each pastry square into bottoms and partially up sides of prepared ramekins. (Pastry should not reach tops of ramekins.) Place ramekins on baking sheet; refrigerate while preparing filling.

2 Heat oil in medium skillet over medium heat. Add onion; cook and stir 2 minutes or until softened and lightly browned. Add garlic; cook and stir 30 seconds. Add roasted pepper, artichokes and spinach; cook and stir 2 minutes or until all liquid has evaporated.

3 Whisk egg yolks, cream cheese, salt and black pepper in medium bowl until well blended. Stir in vegetable mixture and 3 tablespoons Romano cheese.

4 Beat egg whites in large bowl with electric mixer at high speed 3 minutes or until stiff peaks form. Fold into vegetable mixture until blended. Divide mixture evenly among pastry-lined ramekins; sprinkle with remaining 1 tablespoon Romano cheese. Fold corners of pastry towards center.

5 Bake 25 minutes or until crust is golden brown and filling is puffed. Cool in ramekins 2 minutes; remove to wire rack. Serve warm.

STRAWBERRY BANANA FRENCH TOAST

MAKES 2 SERVINGS

1 cup sliced fresh strawberries
  (about 8 medium)

2 teaspoons sugar

2 eggs

½ cup milk

3 tablespoons all-purpose flour

1 teaspoon vanilla

⅛ teaspoon salt

1 tablespoon butter

4 slices (1 inch thick) egg bread
  or country bread

1 banana, cut into ¼-inch slices

Whipped cream and
  powdered sugar (optional)

Maple syrup

1 Combine strawberries and sugar in small bowl; toss to coat. Set aside while preparing French toast.

2 Whisk eggs, milk, flour, vanilla and salt in shallow bowl or pie plate until well blended. Melt ½ tablespoon butter in large skillet over medium-high heat. Working with two slices at a time, dip bread into egg mixture, turning to coat completely; let excess drip off. Add to skillet; cook 3 to 4 minutes per side or until golden brown. Repeat with remaining butter and bread slices.

3 Top each serving with strawberry mixture and banana slices. Garnish with whipped cream and powdered sugar; serve with maple syrup.

SMOKED SALMON OMELET
MAKES 1 SERVING

3 eggs

2 tablespoons milk

1 tablespoon grated Parmesan cheese

Pinch white or black pepper

1 teaspoon butter

2 tablespoons finely chopped red onion, divided

1 ounce smoked salmon, cut into 1- to 2-inch pieces

2 tablespoons sour cream

1 tablespoon water

1 tablespoon capers, rinsed and drained

Finely chopped fresh parsley (optional)

1 Whisk eggs, milk, cheese and pepper in small bowl until well blended.

2 Heat butter in small (6-inch) nonstick skillet over medium-high heat. Pour egg mixture into pan; stir briefly. Let eggs begin to set at edges, then lift edges and tilt skillet, allowing uncooked portion of egg mixture to flow underneath. Cook about 1 minute or until omelet begins to set. Sprinkle 1 tablespoon onion over half of omelet; top with smoked salmon. Fold other half of omelet over filling; cook about 1 minute. Slide omelet onto serving plate.

3 Whisk sour cream and water in small bowl until blended. Drizzle over omelet; top with remaining 1 tablespoon onion, capers and parsley, if desired.

CINNAMON SWIRL COFFEECAKE
MAKES 9 TO 12 SERVINGS

FILLING AND TOPPING
- ⅓ cup all-purpose flour
- ⅓ cup granulated sugar
- ⅓ cup packed brown sugar
- 1½ tablespoons ground cinnamon
- ¼ teaspoon salt
- ⅛ teaspoon ground allspice
- 3 tablespoons melted butter

CAKE
- 2 cups all-purpose flour
- 1½ teaspoons baking powder
- ¾ teaspoon baking soda
- ½ teaspoon salt
- 1¼ cups granulated sugar
- 9 tablespoons butter, softened
- 3 eggs
- ½ cup sour cream
- 2 teaspoons vanilla
- ¾ cup milk

1 Preheat oven to 350°F. Spray 9-inch square baking pan with nonstick cooking spray.

2 For filling, combine ⅓ cup flour, ⅓ cup granulated sugar, brown sugar, cinnamon, ¼ teaspoon salt and allspice in small bowl; mix well. For topping, remove half of flour mixture to another small bowl; stir in melted butter until blended.

3 For cake, combine 2 cups flour, baking powder, baking soda and ½ teaspoon salt in medium bowl; mix well. Combine 1¼ cups granulated sugar and 9 tablespoons butter in large bowl; beat with electric mixer at medium speed 3 minutes or until light and fluffy. Add eggs, sour cream and vanilla; beat until well blended. Scrape down side of bowl. Add flour mixture alternately with milk in two additions, beating at low speed until blended. Spread half of batter in prepared pan; sprinkle evenly with filling. Spread remaining batter over filling with dampened hands. Sprinkle with topping.

4 Bake 45 to 50 minutes or until toothpick inserted into center comes out clean. Cool completely in pan on wire rack.

APPETIZERS

WHITE SPINACH QUESO
MAKES 4 TO 6 SERVINGS

1 tablespoon olive oil

1 clove garlic, minced

1 tablespoon all-purpose flour

1 can (12 ounces) evaporated milk

½ teaspoon salt

2 cups (8 ounces) shredded Monterey Jack cheese, divided

1 package (10 ounces) frozen chopped spinach, thawed and squeezed dry

Optional toppings: pico de gallo, guacamole, chopped fresh cilantro and queso fresco

Tortilla chips

1 Preheat broiler.

2 Heat oil in medium saucepan over medium-low heat. Add garlic; cook and stir 1 minute without browning. Add flour; whisk until smooth. Add evaporated milk in thin steady stream, whisking constantly. Stir in salt. Cook about 4 minutes or until slightly thickened, whisking frequently. Add 1½ cups Monterey Jack cheese; whisk until smooth. Stir in spinach. Pour into medium cast iron skillet; sprinkle with remaining ½ cup Monterey Jack cheese.

3 Broil about 1 minute or until cheese is melted and browned in spots. Top with pico de gallo, guacamole, cilantro and queso fresco. Serve immediately with tortilla chips.

BUFFALO WINGS

MAKES 4 SERVINGS

1 cup hot pepper sauce

⅓ cup vegetable oil, plus additional for frying

1 teaspoon sugar

½ teaspoon garlic powder

½ teaspoon ground red pepper

½ teaspoon Worcestershire sauce

⅛ teaspoon black pepper

1 pound chicken wings, tips discarded, separated at joints

Blue cheese or ranch dressing

Celery sticks

1 Combine hot pepper sauce, ⅓ cup oil, sugar, garlic powder, red pepper, Worcestershire sauce and black pepper in small saucepan; cook over medium heat 20 minutes. Remove from heat; pour sauce into large bowl.

2 Heat 3 inches of oil in large saucepan over medium-high heat to 350°F; adjust heat to maintain temperature. Add wings; cook 10 minutes or until crispy. Drain on wire rack set over paper towels.

3 Transfer wings to bowl of sauce; toss to coat. Serve with blue cheese dressing and celery sticks.

QUATTRO FORMAGGIO FOCACCIA

MAKES 12 SERVINGS

1¼ cups warm water (100° to 105°F)

1 tablespoon sugar

1 package (¼ ounce) rapid rise yeast

1 teaspoon salt

3¼ to 3½ cups all-purpose flour

¼ cup plus 2 tablespoons olive oil, divided

¼ cup marinara sauce with basil

1 cup (4 ounces) shredded Italian cheese blend

1 Combine water, sugar, yeast and salt in large bowl of electric stand mixer; let stand 5 minutes. Stir in 3 cups flour and ¼ cup oil with spoon or spatula. Attach dough hook to mixer; knead at low speed 5 minutes. Place dough in large greased bowl; turn to grease top. Cover and let rise 1 to 1½ hours or until doubled in size.

2 Punch down dough. Pour remaining 2 tablespoons oil into 13×9-inch baking pan; pat and stretch dough to fill pan. Dimple top of dough all over with fingers.

3 Spread marinara sauce evenly over dough; sprinkle with cheese. Cover and let rise 30 minutes or until puffy. Preheat oven to 425°F.

4 Bake 17 to 20 minutes or until golden brown. Cut focaccia into squares or strips to serve.

GUACAMOLE

MAKES 2 CUPS

2 large ripe avocados
2 teaspoons fresh lime juice
¼ cup finely chopped red onion
2 tablespoons chopped fresh
cilantro

½ jalapeño pepper,* finely
chopped
½ teaspoon salt

*Jalapeño peppers can sting and
irritate the skin, so wear rubber
gloves when handling peppers
and do not touch your eyes.*

1 Cut avocados in half lengthwise around pits. Remove pits. Scoop
avocados into large bowl; sprinkle with lime juice and toss to coat.
Mash to desired consistency with fork or potato masher.

2 Add onion, cilantro, jalapeño and salt; stir gently until well blended.
Taste and add additional salt, if desired.

MOZZARELLA STICKS

MAKES 4 TO 6 SERVINGS

¼ cup all-purpose flour

2 eggs

1 tablespoon water

1 cup plain dry bread crumbs

2 teaspoons Italian seasoning

½ teaspoon salt

½ teaspoon garlic powder

1 package (12 ounces) string
cheese (12 sticks)

Vegetable oil for frying

1 cup marinara or pizza sauce,
heated

1 Place flour in shallow bowl. Whisk eggs and water in another shallow bowl. Combine bread crumbs, Italian seasoning, salt and garlic powder in third shallow bowl.

2 Coat each piece of cheese with flour. Dip in egg mixture, letting excess drip back into bowl. Roll in bread crumb mixture to coat. Dip again in egg mixture and roll again in bread crumb mixture. Place on plate; refrigerate until ready to cook.

3 Heat 2 inches of oil in large saucepan over medium-high heat to 350°F; adjust heat to maintain temperature. Add cheese sticks; cook about 1 minute or until golden brown. Drain on wire rack. Serve with warm marinara sauce for dipping.

CHICKEN PARMESAN SLIDERS

MAKES 12 SLIDERS

4 boneless skinless chicken breasts (6 to 8 ounces each)

¼ cup all-purpose flour

2 eggs

1 tablespoon water

1 cup Italian-seasoned dry bread crumbs

½ cup grated Parmesan cheese

Salt and black pepper

Olive oil

12 slider buns (about 3 inches), split

¾ cup marinara sauce

6 tablespoons Alfredo sauce

6 slices mozzarella cheese, cut into halves

2 tablespoons butter, melted

¼ teaspoon garlic powder

6 tablespoons pesto

1 Preheat oven to 375°F. Line baking sheet with foil; top with wire rack.

2 Use rolling pin or meat mallet to pound chicken to ½-inch thickness between two sheets of plastic wrap. Cut each chicken breast into three pieces about the size of slider buns.

3 Place flour in shallow dish. Whisk eggs and water in second shallow dish. Combine bread crumbs and Parmesan in third shallow dish. Season flour and egg mixture with pinch of salt and pepper. Coat chicken pieces lightly with flour, shaking off excess. Dip in egg mixture, coating completely; roll in bread crumb mixture to coat. Place on large plate; let stand 10 minutes.

4 Heat ¼ inch oil in large nonstick skillet over medium-high heat. Add chicken in single layer (cook in two batches if necessary); cook 3 to 4 minutes per side or until golden brown. Remove chicken to wire rack; bake 5 minutes or until no longer pink in center. Remove rack with chicken from baking sheet.

5 Arrange slider buns on foil-lined baking sheet with bottoms cut sides up and tops cut sides down. Spread 1 tablespoon marinara sauce over each bottom bun; top with piece of chicken. Spread ½ tablespoon Alfredo sauce over chicken; top with half slice mozzarella. Combine butter and garlic powder in small bowl; brush mixture over top buns.

6 Bake 3 to 4 minutes or until mozzarella is melted and top buns are lightly toasted. Spread ½ tablespoon pesto over mozzarella; cover with top buns.

TEX-MEX NACHOS
MAKES 4 TO 6 SERVINGS

1 tablespoon vegetable oil

8 ounces ground beef

½ cup chopped onion

2 cloves garlic, minced

2 teaspoons chili powder

1 teaspoon ground cumin

½ teaspoon salt

½ teaspoon dried oregano

1 can (about 15 ounces) kidney beans, rinsed and drained

½ cup corn

½ cup sour cream, divided

2 tablespoons mayonnaise

1 tablespoon lime juice

¼ to ½ teaspoon chipotle chili powder

½ (14-ounce) bag tortilla chips

½ (15-ounce) jar Cheddar cheese dip, warmed

½ cup pico de gallo

¼ cup guacamole

1 cup shredded iceberg lettuce

2 jalapeño peppers,* thinly sliced into rings

Jalapeño peppers can sting and irritate the skin, so wear rubber gloves when handling peppers and do not touch your eyes.

1 Heat oil in large skillet over medium-high heat. Add beef, onion and garlic; cook and stir 6 minutes or until beef is no longer pink. Add chili powder, cumin, salt and oregano; cook and stir 1 minute. Add beans and corn; reduce heat to medium-low and cook 3 minutes or until heated through.

2 For chipotle sauce, combine ¼ cup sour cream, mayonnaise, lime juice and chipotle chili powder in small bowl; mix well. Place in small plastic squeeze bottle.

3 Spread tortilla chips on platter or large plate. Top with beef mixture; drizzle with cheese dip. Top with pico de gallo, guacamole, remaining ¼ cup sour cream, lettuce and jalapeños. Squeeze chipotle sauce over nachos. Serve immediately.

BUFFALO CAULIFLOWER
MAKES 8 SERVINGS

¾ cup all-purpose flour
¼ cup cornstarch
1 teaspoon salt
½ teaspoon garlic powder
¼ teaspoon black pepper
1 cup water

1 large head cauliflower
  (2½ pounds), cut into
  1-inch florets
½ cup hot pepper sauce
¼ cup (½ stick) butter, melted
Blue cheese or ranch dressing
  and celery sticks for serving

1 Preheat oven to 450°F. Line baking sheet with foil; spray with nonstick cooking spray.

2 Whisk flour, cornstarch, salt, garlic powder and pepper in large bowl. Whisk in water until smooth and well blended. Add cauliflower to batter in batches; stir to coat. Arrange on prepared baking sheet.

3 Bake 20 minutes or until cauliflower is lightly browned. Combine hot pepper sauce and butter in small bowl; mix well. Pour over cauliflower; toss until well blended.

4 Bake 5 minutes; stir. Bake 5 minutes more or until cauliflower is glazed and crisp. Serve with blue cheese dressing and celery sticks.

SPINACH FLORENTINE FLATBREAD
MAKES 8 SERVINGS

1 tablespoon olive oil

2 cloves garlic, minced

1 package (10 ounces) baby spinach

1 can (about 14 ounces) quartered artichoke hearts, drained and sliced

½ teaspoon salt

¼ teaspoon dried oregano

Black pepper

Red pepper flakes

2 rectangular pizza or flatbread crusts (about 8 ounces each)

1 plum tomato, seeded and diced

2 cups (8 ounces) shredded Monterey Jack cheese

½ cup (2 ounces) shredded Italian cheese blend

1 Preheat oven to 425°F.

2 Heat oil in large nonstick skillet over medium-high heat. Add garlic; cook and stir 30 seconds. Add half of spinach; cook and stir until slightly wilted. Add additional spinach by handfuls; cook about 3 minutes or until completely wilted, stirring occasionally. Transfer to medium bowl; stir in artichokes, salt and oregano. Season with black pepper and red pepper flakes.

3 Place pizza crusts on large baking sheet. Spread spinach mixture over crusts; sprinkle with tomato, Monterey Jack cheese and Italian cheese blend.

4 Bake 12 minutes or until cheeses are melted and edges of crusts are browned.

TIP

For crispier crusts, bake flatbreads on a preheated pizza stone or directly on the oven rack.

CHICKEN LETTUCE WRAPS
MAKES 6 TO 8 SERVINGS

1 tablespoon vegetable oil

1 small onion, finely chopped

5 ounces cremini mushrooms, finely chopped (about 2 cups)

1 pound ground chicken

¼ cup hoisin sauce

2 tablespoons soy sauce

1 tablespoon rice vinegar

1 tablespoon sriracha sauce

1 tablespoon oyster sauce

2 cloves garlic, minced

1 teaspoon grated fresh ginger

1 teaspoon dark sesame oil

½ cup finely chopped water chestnuts

2 green onions, thinly sliced

1 head butter lettuce

1 Heat oil in large skillet over medium-high heat. Add onion; cook and stir 2 minutes. Add mushrooms; cook about 8 minutes or until lightly browned and liquid has evaporated, stirring occasionally.

2 Add chicken; cook about 8 minutes or until no longer pink, stirring to break up meat. Stir in hoisin sauce, soy sauce, vinegar, sriracha, oyster sauce, garlic, ginger and sesame oil; cook 4 minutes. Add water chestnuts; cook and stir 2 minutes or until heated through. Remove from heat; stir in green onions.

3 Separate lettuce leaves. Spoon about ¼ cup chicken mixture into each lettuce leaf. Serve immediately.

POTATO SKINS

MAKES 6 TO 8 SERVINGS

8 medium baking potatoes (6 to 8 ounces each), unpeeled

1 tablespoon vegetable oil

1 teaspoon salt

⅛ teaspoon black pepper

1 tablespoon butter, melted

1 cup (4 ounces) shredded Cheddar cheese

8 slices bacon, crisp-cooked and coarsely chopped

1 cup sour cream

3 tablespoons snipped fresh chives

1 Preheat oven to 400°F.

2 Prick potatoes all over with fork. Rub oil over potatoes; sprinkle with salt and pepper. Place in 13×9-inch baking pan. Bake 1 hour or until fork-tender. Let stand until cool enough to handle. *Reduce oven temperature to 350°F.*

3 Cut potatoes in half lengthwise; cut small slice off bottom of each half so potato halves lay flat. Scoop out soft middles of potato halves; reserve for another use. Place potato halves, skin sides up, in baking pan; brush potato skins with butter.

4 Bake 20 to 25 minutes or until crisp. Turn potatoes over; top with cheese and bacon. Bake 5 minutes or until cheese is melted. Cool slightly. Top with sour cream and chives just before serving.

PRETZEL NUGGETS

MAKES 12 SERVINGS

½ cup mayonnaise

3 tablespoons honey

3 tablespoons Dijon mustard

1 tablespoon yellow mustard

⅛ teaspoon paprika

1⅔ cups warm water (110° to 115°F)

1 package (¼ ounce) active dry yeast

2 teaspoons sugar

½ teaspoon salt

4½ cups all-purpose flour, plus additional for work surface

2 tablespoons butter, softened

12 cups water

½ cup baking soda

Kosher salt

1 For honey mustard dip, combine mayonnaise, honey, Dijon mustard, yellow mustard and paprika in small bowl; mix well. Cover and refrigerate until ready to use.

2 Whisk 1⅔ cups warm water, yeast, sugar and ½ teaspoon salt in large bowl of electric stand mixer; let stand 5 minutes or until bubbly.

3 Add 4½ cups flour and butter to yeast mixture; beat at low speed until blended, scraping side of bowl occasionally. Replace paddle attachment with dough hook; knead at medium speed 5 minutes.

4 Place dough in large greased bowl; turn to grease top. Cover and let rise in warm place 1 hour or until doubled in size.

5 Preheat oven to 450°F. Line baking sheets with foil; spray with nonstick cooking spray. Punch down dough; transfer to floured work surface. Flatten and stretch dough into 12 pieces. Roll each piece into 12-inch-long rope; cut each rope into 8 equal pieces.

6 Bring 12 cups water to a boil in large saucepan over high heat. Stir in baking soda until dissolved. Working in batches, drop dough pieces into boiling water; boil 30 seconds. Remove to prepared baking sheets with slotted spoon; sprinkle with kosher salt.

7 Bake 12 minutes or until dark golden brown, rotating baking sheets halfway through. Serve with honey mustard dip.

SOUPS

CLASSIC FRENCH ONION SOUP
MAKES 4 SERVINGS

3 tablespoons butter

3 large yellow onions (about 2 pounds), sliced

3 cans (about 14 ounces each) beef broth

½ cup dry sherry

½ teaspoon salt

½ teaspoon dried thyme

¼ teaspoon white pepper

4 slices French bread

1 cup (4 ounces) shredded Swiss cheese

1 Melt butter in large saucepan or Dutch oven over medium-high heat. Add onions; cook 15 minutes or until lightly browned, stirring occasionally. Reduce heat to medium; cook 30 to 40 minutes until onions are deep golden brown, stirring occasionally.

2 Stir in broth, sherry, salt, thyme and pepper; bring to a boil. Reduce heat to low; cook 20 minutes. Preheat broiler.

3 Ladle soup into four heatproof bowls; top with bread slice and cheese. Broil 4 inches from heat 2 to 3 minutes or until cheese is bubbly and browned.

HEARTY TUSCAN SOUP

MAKES 6 TO 8 SERVINGS

1 teaspoon olive oil

1 pound bulk mild or hot Italian sausage*

1 medium onion, chopped

3 cloves garlic, minced

¼ cup all-purpose flour

5 cups chicken broth

1 teaspoon salt

½ teaspoon Italian seasoning

3 medium unpeeled russet potatoes (about 1 pound), halved lengthwise and thinly sliced

2 cups packed torn stemmed kale leaves

1 cup half-and-half or whipping cream

Or use sausage links and remove from casings.

1 Heat oil in large saucepan or Dutch oven over medium-high heat. Add sausage; cook until sausage begins to brown, stirring to break up meat. Add onion and garlic; cook about 5 minutes or until onion is softened and sausage is browned, stirring occasionally.

2 Stir in flour until blended. Add broth, salt and Italian seasoning; bring to a boil. Stir in potatoes and kale. Reduce heat to medium-low; cook 15 to 20 minutes or until potatoes are fork-tender.

3 Reduce heat to low; stir in half-and-half. Cook about 5 minutes or until heated through.

CHICKEN ENCHILADA SOUP
MAKES 8 TO 10 SERVINGS

2 tablespoons vegetable oil, divided

1½ pounds boneless skinless chicken breasts, cut into ½-inch cubes

½ cup chopped onion

2 cloves garlic, minced

2 cans (about 14 ounces each) chicken broth

3 cups water, divided

1 cup masa harina

1 package (16 ounces) pasteurized process cheese product, cubed

1 can (10 ounces) mild red enchilada sauce

1 teaspoon chili powder

½ teaspoon salt

½ teaspoon ground cumin

1 medium tomato, seeded and chopped

Crispy tortilla strips*

*If tortilla strips are not available, crumble tortilla chips into bite-size pieces.

1 Heat 1 tablespoon oil in large saucepan or Dutch oven over medium-high heat. Add chicken; cook and stir 10 minutes or until no longer pink. Transfer to large bowl with slotted spoon; drain fat from saucepan.

2 Heat remaining 1 tablespoon oil in same saucepan over medium-high heat. Add onion and garlic; cook and stir 3 minutes or until softened. Stir in broth.

3 Whisk 2 cups water into masa harina in large bowl until smooth. Whisk mixture into broth in saucepan. Stir in cheese product, remaining 1 cup water, enchilada sauce, chili powder, salt and cumin; bring to a boil over high heat. Add chicken. Reduce heat to medium-low; cook 30 minutes, stirring frequently. Ladle soup into bowls; top with tomatoes and tortilla strips.

BLACK BEAN SOUP

MAKES 4 TO 6 SERVINGS

2 tablespoons vegetable oil

1 cup diced onion

1 stalk celery, diced

2 carrots, diced

½ small green bell pepper, diced

4 cloves garlic, minced

4 cans (about 15 ounces each) black beans, rinsed and drained, divided

4 cups (32 ounces) chicken or vegetable broth, divided

2 tablespoons cider vinegar

2 teaspoons chili powder

½ teaspoon salt

½ teaspoon ground red pepper

½ teaspoon ground cumin

¼ teaspoon liquid smoke

Garnishes: sour cream, chopped green onions and shredded Cheddar cheese

1 Heat oil in large saucepan or Dutch oven over medium-low heat. Add onion, celery, carrots, bell pepper and garlic; cook 10 minutes, stirring occasionally.

2 Combine half of beans and 1 cup broth in food processor or blender; process until smooth. Add to vegetables in saucepan.

3 Stir in remaining beans, remaining 3 cups broth, vinegar, chili powder, salt, red pepper, cumin and liquid smoke; bring to a boil over high heat. Reduce heat to medium-low; cook 1 hour or until vegetables are tender and soup is thickened. Garnish as desired.

PASTA FAGIOLI

MAKES 8 SERVINGS

2 tablespoons olive oil, divided
1 pound ground beef
1 cup chopped onion
1 cup diced carrots (about 2 medium)
1 cup diced celery (about 2 stalks)
3 cloves garlic, minced
4 cups beef broth
1 can (28 ounces) diced tomatoes
1 can (15 ounces) tomato sauce
1 tablespoon cider vinegar
2 teaspoons sugar
1½ teaspoons dried basil
1¼ teaspoons salt
1 teaspoon dried oregano
¾ teaspoon dried thyme
2 cups uncooked ditalini pasta
1 can (about 15 ounces) dark red kidney beans, rinsed and drained
1 can (about 15 ounces) cannellini beans, rinsed and drained
Grated Romano cheese

1 Heat 1 tablespoon oil in large saucepan or Dutch oven over medium-high heat. Add beef; cook 5 minutes or until browned, stirring to break up meat. Transfer to medium bowl; set aside. Drain fat from saucepan.

2 Heat remaining 1 tablespoon oil in same saucepan over medium-high heat. Add onion, carrots and celery; cook and stir 5 minutes or until vegetables are tender. Add garlic; cook and stir 1 minute. Add cooked beef, broth, tomatoes, tomato sauce, vinegar, sugar, basil, salt, oregano and thyme; bring to a boil. Reduce heat to medium-low; cover and simmer 30 minutes.

3 Add pasta, kidney beans and cannellini beans; cook over medium heat 10 minutes or until pasta is tender, stirring frequently. Ladle into bowls; top with cheese.

CREAMY TOMATO SOUP

MAKES 6 SERVINGS

3 tablespoons olive oil, divided
2 tablespoons butter
1 large onion, finely chopped
2 cloves garlic, minced
2 teaspoons sugar
1 teaspoon salt
½ teaspoon dried oregano

2 cans (28 ounces each) peeled Italian plum tomatoes, undrained
4 cups ½-inch focaccia cubes (half of 9-ounce loaf)
½ teaspoon freshly ground black pepper
½ cup whipping cream

1 Heat 2 tablespoons oil and butter in large saucepan over medium-high heat. Add onion; cook and stir 5 minutes or until softened. Add garlic, sugar, salt and oregano; cook and stir 30 seconds. Stir in tomatoes with juice; bring to a boil. Reduce heat to medium-low; simmer 45 minutes, stirring occasionally.

2 Meanwhile, prepare croutons. Preheat oven to 350°F. Combine focaccia cubes, remaining 1 tablespoon oil and pepper in large bowl; toss to coat. Spread on large rimmed baking sheet. Bake about 10 minutes or until bread cubes are golden brown.

3 Blend soup with hand-held immersion blender until smooth. (Or process soup in batches in food processor or blender.) Stir in cream; cook until heated through. Serve soup topped with croutons.

ITALIAN WEDDING SOUP
MAKES 8 SERVINGS

MEATBALLS

- 2 eggs
- 2 cloves garlic, minced
- 1 teaspoon salt
- ⅛ teaspoon black pepper
- 1½ pounds meat loaf mix (ground beef and pork)
- ¾ cup plain dry bread crumbs
- ½ cup grated Parmesan cheese

SOUP

- 2 tablespoons olive oil
- 1 onion, chopped
- 2 carrots, chopped
- 4 cloves garlic, minced
- 2 heads escarole or curly endive, coarsely chopped
- 8 cups chicken broth
- 1 can (about 14 ounces) Italian plum tomatoes, undrained, coarsely chopped
- 3 fresh thyme sprigs
- 1 teaspoon salt
- ½ teaspoon red pepper flakes
- 1 cup uncooked acini di pepe pasta

1 For meatballs, beat eggs, 2 cloves garlic, 1 teaspoon salt and black pepper in large bowl until blended. Stir in meat loaf mix, bread crumbs and cheese; mix gently until well blended. Shape mixture by tablespoonfuls into 1-inch balls.

2 Heat oil in large saucepan or Dutch oven over medium heat. Cook meatballs in batches 5 minutes or until browned. Remove to plate; set aside.

3 Add onion, carrots and 4 cloves garlic to saucepan; cook and stir 5 minutes or until onion is lightly browned. Add escarole; cook 2 minutes or until wilted. Stir in broth, tomatoes with juice, thyme, 1 teaspoon salt and red pepper flakes; bring to a boil over high heat. Reduce heat to medium-low; simmer 15 minutes.

4 Add meatballs and pasta to soup; return to a boil over high heat. Reduce heat to medium; cook 10 minutes or until pasta is tender. Remove and discard thyme sprigs before serving.

HOT AND SOUR SOUP

MAKES 4 TO 6 SERVINGS

1 package (1 ounce) dried shiitake mushrooms

4 ounces firm tofu, drained

4 cups chicken broth

3 tablespoons white vinegar

2 tablespoons soy sauce

½ to 1 teaspoon hot chili oil

1 teaspoon white pepper, divided

1 cup shredded cooked chicken

½ cup drained canned bamboo shoots, cut into thin strips

3 tablespoons water

2 tablespoons cornstarch

1 egg white, lightly beaten

2 tablespoons balsamic vinegar

1 teaspoon dark sesame oil

¼ cup thinly sliced green onions (optional)

1 Place mushrooms in small bowl; cover with warm water and let stand 20 minutes to soften. Drain mushrooms; squeeze out excess water. Discard stems; slice caps. Press tofu lightly between paper towels; cut into ½-inch cubes.

2 Combine broth, white vinegar, soy sauce, chili oil and ½ teaspoon white pepper in large saucepan; bring to a boil over high heat. Reduce heat to medium-low; cook 2 minutes. Add mushrooms, tofu, chicken and bamboo shoots; cook and stir 5 minutes or until heated through.

3 Stir water into cornstarch in small bowl until smooth. Stir into soup; cook 4 minutes or until soup boils and thickens, stirring frequently.

4 Remove from heat. Stirring constantly in one direction, slowly pour egg white in thin stream into soup. Stir in balsamic vinegar, sesame oil and remaining ½ teaspoon white pepper. Garnish with green onions.

SAUSAGE RICE SOUP

MAKES 4 TO 6 SERVINGS

2 teaspoons olive oil

8 ounces Italian sausage links, casings removed

1 small onion, chopped

½ teaspoon fennel seeds

1 tablespoon tomato paste

4 cups chicken broth

1 can (about 14 ounces) whole tomatoes, undrained, tomatoes crushed with hands or chopped

1½ cups water

½ cup uncooked rice

¼ teaspoon salt

⅛ teaspoon black pepper

2 to 3 ounces baby spinach

⅓ cup shredded mozzarella cheese (optional)

1 Heat oil in large saucepan or Dutch oven over medium-high heat. Add sausage; cook about 8 minutes or until browned, stirring to break up meat into bite-size pieces. Add onion; cook and stir 5 minutes or until softened. Add fennel seeds; cook and stir 30 seconds. Add tomato paste; cook and stir 1 minute.

2 Stir in broth, tomatoes with juice, water, rice, ¼ teaspoon salt and ⅛ teaspoon pepper; bring to a boil. Reduce heat to medium-low; simmer about 18 minutes or until rice is tender. Stir in spinach; cook about 3 minutes or until wilted. Season with additional salt and pepper.

3 Sprinkle with cheese, if desired, just before serving.

SUMMER CORN CHOWDER

MAKES 6 SERVINGS

5 ears corn, shucked

2 tablespoons butter

1 medium onion, chopped

1 large poblano pepper, diced (¼-inch pieces)

2 cloves garlic, minced

1 container (32 ounces) chicken or vegetable broth

1½ teaspoons salt, divided

½ teaspoon black pepper, divided

¼ teaspoon ground red pepper

1 pound red potatoes, peeled and cut into ½-inch pieces

3 plum tomatoes, diced (about 2 cups)

½ cup whipping cream

2 tablespoons lime juice

2 tablespoons chopped fresh cilantro

¼ cup crumbled crisp-cooked bacon (optional)

1 Cut kernels off cobs; place in medium bowl. Working over bowl, run back of knife up and down cobs to release additional corn pulp and milk from cobs into bowl. Break cobs in half; set aside.

2 Melt butter in large saucepan or Dutch oven over medium heat. Add onion, poblano pepper and garlic; cook about 5 minutes or until vegetables are softened, stirring occasionally. Stir in broth, 1 teaspoon salt, ¼ teaspoon black pepper and red pepper; mix well. Add corn cobs; bring to a boil. Reduce heat to medium-low; cover and cook 15 minutes.

3 Stir in potatoes; cover and cook 20 minutes. Stir in corn and tomatoes; cook, uncovered, 20 minutes. Remove and discard corn cobs. Coarsely mash soup with potato masher. (Or use immersion blender to briefly blend soup just until slightly chunky.)

4 Stir in cream; cook 3 minutes or until heated through. Stir in lime juice and cilantro. Garnish with bacon.

SALADS

CHICKEN WALDORF SALAD
MAKES 4 SERVINGS

DRESSING
- ⅓ cup balsamic vinegar
- 2 tablespoons Dijon mustard
- 2 teaspoons minced garlic
- ½ teaspoon salt
- ¼ teaspoon black pepper
- ⅔ cup extra virgin olive oil

SALAD
- 8 cups mixed greens
- 1 large Granny Smith apple, cut into ½-inch pieces
- ⅔ cup diced celery
- ⅔ cup halved red seedless grapes
- 12 to 16 ounces sliced grilled chicken breasts
- ½ cup candied walnuts
- ½ cup crumbled blue cheese

1 For dressing, combine vinegar, mustard, garlic, salt and pepper in medium bowl; mix well. Slowly whisk in oil in thin, steady stream until well blended.

2 For salad, combine mixed greens, apple, celery and grapes in large bowl. Add half of dressing; toss to coat. Top with chicken, walnuts and cheese; drizzle with additional dressing.

STEAKHOUSE CHOPPED SALAD
MAKES 8 TO 10 SERVINGS

DRESSING

Italian Seasoning Mix (recipe follows) *or* 1 package (about 2 tablespoons) Italian salad dressing mix

⅓ cup white balsamic vinegar

¼ cup Dijon mustard

⅔ cup extra virgin olive oil

SALAD

1 medium head iceberg lettuce, chopped

1 medium head romaine lettuce, chopped

1 can (about 14 ounces) hearts of palm or artichoke hearts, quartered lengthwise then sliced crosswise

1 large avocado, diced

1½ cups crumbled blue cheese

2 hard-cooked eggs, chopped

1 ripe tomato, chopped

½ small red onion, finely chopped

12 slices bacon, crisp-cooked and crumbled

1 For dressing, prepare Italian Seasoning mix. Whisk vinegar, mustard and dressing mix in small bowl. Slowly whisk in oil in thin, steady stream until well blended. Set aside until ready to use. (Dressing can be made up to 1 week in advance; refrigerate in jar with tight-fitting lid.)

2 For salad, combine lettuce, hearts of palm, avocado, cheese, eggs, tomato, onion and bacon in large bowl. Add dressing; toss to coat.

ITALIAN SEASONING MIX
MAKES ABOUT 2½ TABLESPOONS

1½ teaspoons salt

1½ teaspoons dried oregano

¾ teaspoon sugar

¾ teaspoon onion powder

¾ teaspoon dried parsley flakes

½ teaspoon garlic powder

¼ teaspoon dried basil

¼ teaspoon black pepper

⅛ teaspoon dried thyme

⅛ teaspoon celery salt

Combine all ingredients in small bowl; mix well.

TACO SALAD SUPREME

MAKES 4 SERVINGS

CHILI

- 1 pound ground beef
- 1 medium onion, chopped
- 1 stalk celery, chopped
- 2 medium fresh tomatoes, chopped
- 1 jalapeño pepper,* finely chopped
- 1½ teaspoons chili powder
- 1 teaspoon salt
- 1 teaspoon ground cumin
- ½ teaspoon black pepper
- 1 can (15 ounces) tomato sauce
- 1 can (about 15 ounces) kidney beans, rinsed and drained
- 1 can (about 15 ounces) pinto beans, rinsed and drained
- 1 cup water

SALAD

- 8 cups chopped romaine lettuce (large pieces)
- 2 cups diced fresh tomatoes
- 48 small round tortilla chips
- 1 cup salsa
- ½ cup sour cream
- 1 cup (4 ounces) shredded Cheddar cheese

Jalapeño peppers can sting and irritate the skin, so wear rubber gloves when handling peppers and do not touch your eyes.

1 For chili, combine beef, onion and celery in large saucepan; cook over medium-high heat 6 to 8 minutes or until beef is no longer pink, stirring to break up meat. Drain fat.

2 Add chopped tomatoes, jalapeño, chili powder, salt, cumin and black pepper; cook and stir 1 minute. Stir in tomato sauce, beans and water; bring to a boil. Reduce heat to medium-low; cook about 1 hour or until most of liquid is absorbed.

3 For each salad, combine 2 cups lettuce and ½ cup diced tomatoes in individual bowl. Top with 12 tortilla chips, ¾ cup chili, ¼ cup salsa and 2 tablespoons sour cream. Sprinkle with ¼ cup cheese. (Reserve remaining chili for another use.)

COLESLAW

MAKES 10 SERVINGS

1 medium head green cabbage, shredded

1 medium carrot, shredded

½ cup mayonnaise

½ cup milk

⅓ cup sugar

3 tablespoons lemon juice

1½ tablespoons white vinegar

½ teaspoon salt

⅛ teaspoon black pepper

1 Combine cabbage and carrot in large bowl; mix well.

2 Combine mayonnaise, milk, sugar, lemon juice, vinegar, salt and pepper in medium bowl; whisk until well blended. Add to cabbage mixture; stir until blended.

SALADS

GARBAGE SALAD

MAKES 4 TO 6 SERVINGS

DRESSING

- ⅓ cup red wine vinegar
- 2 cloves garlic, minced
- 2 teaspoons sugar
- 1 teaspoon Italian seasoning
- ¼ teaspoon salt
- ¼ teaspoon black pepper
- ⅓ cup vegetable or canola oil

SALAD

- 1 package (5 ounces) spring mix
- 5 leaves romaine lettuce, chopped
- 1 small cucumber, diced
- 2 small plum tomatoes, diced
- ½ red onion, thinly sliced
- ¼ cup pitted kalamata olives
- 4 radishes, thinly sliced
- 4 ounces thinly sliced Genoa salami, cut into ¼-inch strips
- 4 ounces provolone cheese, cut into ¼-inch strips
- ¼ cup grated Parmesan cheese

1 For dressing, whisk vinegar, garlic, sugar, Italian seasoning, salt and pepper in small bowl until blended. Slowly whisk in oil in thin, steady stream until well blended.

2 Combine spring mix, romaine, cucumber, tomatoes, onion, olives and radishes in large bowl. Add half of dressing; toss gently to coat. Top with salami and provolone; sprinkle with Parmesan. Serve with remaining dressing.

ROASTED BRUSSELS SPROUTS SALAD

MAKES 6 SERVINGS

ROASTED BRUSSELS SPROUTS

- 1 pound brussels sprouts, trimmed and halved
- 2 tablespoons olive oil
- ½ teaspoon salt

SALAD

- 2 cups coarsely chopped baby kale
- 2 cups coarsely chopped romaine lettuce
- 1½ cups candied pecans
- 1 cup halved red grapes
- 1 cup diced cucumbers
- ½ cup dried cranberries
- ½ cup fresh blueberries
- ½ cup chopped red onion
- ¼ cup toasted pumpkin seeds (pepitas)
- 1 container (4 ounces) crumbled goat cheese

DRESSING

- ½ cup olive oil
- 6 tablespoons balsamic vinegar
- 6 tablespoons strawberry jam
- 2 teaspoons Dijon mustard
- 1 teaspoon salt

1 For brussels sprouts, preheat oven to 400°F. Spray large baking sheet with nonstick cooking spray.

2 Combine brussels sprouts, 2 tablespoons oil and ½ teaspoon salt in medium bowl; toss to coat. Arrange brussels sprouts in single layer, cut sides down, on prepared baking sheet. Roast 20 minutes or until tender and browned, stirring once halfway through roasting. Cool completely on baking sheet.

3 For salad, combine kale, lettuce, pecans, grapes, cucumbers, cranberries, blueberries, red onion and pumpkin seeds in large bowl. Top with brussels sprouts and cheese.

4 For dressing, whisk ½ cup oil, vinegar, jam, mustard and 1 teaspoon salt in small bowl until well blended. Pour over salad; toss gently to blend.

SHRIMP AND SPINACH SALAD

MAKES 4 SERVINGS

DRESSING

- 3 to 4 slices bacon
- ¼ cup red wine vinegar
- ½ teaspoon cornstarch
- ¼ cup olive oil
- ¼ cup sugar
- ¼ teaspoon salt
- ¼ teaspoon black pepper
- ¼ teaspoon liquid smoke

SHRIMP

- 2 teaspoons black pepper
- 1 teaspoon salt
- 1 teaspoon garlic powder
- ½ teaspoon sugar
- ½ teaspoon onion powder
- ½ teaspoon ground sage
- ½ teaspoon paprika
- 20 to 24 large raw shrimp, peeled and deveined
- 2 tablespoons olive oil

SALAD

- 8 cups packed torn stemmed spinach
- 1 tomato, diced
- ½ red onion, thinly sliced
- ½ cup sliced roasted red peppers

1 For dressing, cook bacon in large skillet over medium heat until crisp. Drain on paper towel-lined plate. Drain all but 3 tablespoons drippings from skillet. Crumble bacon; set aside.

2 Heat skillet with drippings over medium heat. Stir vinegar into cornstarch in small bowl until smooth. Whisk cornstarch mixture into drippings in skillet; cook 1 to 2 minutes or until slightly thickened, whisking constantly. Remove from heat; pour into small bowl or glass measuring cup. Whisk in ¼ cup oil, ¼ cup sugar, ¼ teaspoon salt, ¼ teaspoon black pepper and liquid smoke until well blended. Wipe out skillet with paper towel.

3 For shrimp, combine 2 teaspoons black pepper, 1 teaspoon salt, garlic powder, ½ teaspoon sugar, onion powder, sage and paprika in medium bowl; mix well. Add shrimp; toss to coat.

4 Heat 2 tablespoons oil in same skillet over medium-high heat. Add shrimp; cook 2 to 3 minutes per side or until shrimp are pink and opaque.

5 For salad, combine spinach, tomato, onion and roasted peppers in large bowl. Add two thirds of dressing; toss to coat. Top with shrimp and crumbled bacon; serve with remaining dressing.

WEDGE SALAD
MAKES 4 SERVINGS

DRESSING
- ¾ cup mayonnaise
- ½ cup buttermilk
- 1 cup crumbled blue cheese, divided
- 1 clove garlic, minced
- ½ teaspoon sugar
- ⅛ teaspoon onion powder
- ⅛ teaspoon salt
- ⅛ teaspoon ground black pepper

SALAD
- 1 head iceberg lettuce
- 1 large tomato, diced (about 1 cup)
- ½ small red onion, cut into thin rings
- ½ cup crumbled crisp-cooked bacon (6 to 8 slices)

1 For dressing, combine mayonnaise, buttermilk, ½ cup cheese, garlic, sugar, onion powder, salt and pepper in food processor or blender; process until smooth.

2 For salad, cut lettuce into quarters through stem end; remove stem from each wedge. Place wedges on individual serving plates; top with dressing. Sprinkle with tomato, onion, remaining ½ cup cheese and bacon.

BBQ CHICKEN SALAD

MAKES 4 SERVINGS

DRESSING

- ¾ cup light or regular mayonnaise
- ⅓ cup buttermilk
- ¼ cup sour cream
- 1 tablespoon white wine vinegar
- 1 teaspoon sugar
- ¼ teaspoon salt
- ¼ teaspoon garlic powder
- ¼ teaspoon onion powder
- ¼ teaspoon dried parsley flakes
- ¼ teaspoon dried dill weed
- ¼ teaspoon black pepper

SALAD

- 12 to 16 ounces grilled chicken breast strips
- ½ cup barbecue sauce
- 4 cups chopped romaine lettuce
- 4 cups chopped iceberg lettuce
- 2 medium tomatoes, seeded and chopped
- ¾ cup canned or thawed frozen corn, drained
- ¾ cup diced jicama
- ¾ cup (3 ounces) shredded Monterey Jack cheese
- ¼ cup chopped fresh cilantro
- 2 green onions, sliced
- 1 cup crispy tortilla strips*

If tortilla strips are unavailable, crumble tortilla chips into bite-size pieces.

1 For dressing, whisk mayonnaise, buttermilk, sour cream, vinegar, sugar, salt, garlic powder, onion powder, parsley flakes, dill weed and pepper in medium bowl until well blended. Cover and refrigerate until ready to serve.

2 For salad, cut chicken strips into ½-inch pieces. Combine chicken and barbecue sauce in medium bowl; toss to coat.

3 Combine lettuce, tomatoes, corn, jicama, cheese and cilantro in large bowl. Add two thirds of dressing; toss to coat. Add remaining dressing, if necessary. Divide salad among four plates; top with chicken, green onions and tortilla strips.

AMAZING APPLE SALAD
MAKES 4 SERVINGS

DRESSING

- 5 tablespoons apple juice concentrate
- ¼ cup white balsamic vinegar
- 1 tablespoon lemon juice
- 1 tablespoon sugar
- 1 clove garlic, minced
- ½ teaspoon salt
- ½ teaspoon onion powder
- ¼ teaspoon ground ginger
- ¼ cup extra virgin olive oil

SALAD

- 12 cups mixed greens such as chopped romaine lettuce and spring greens
- 12 ounces thinly sliced cooked chicken
- 2 tomatoes, cut into wedges
- 1 package (about 3 ounces) dried apple chips
- ½ red onion, thinly sliced
- ½ cup crumbled gorgonzola or blue cheese
- ½ cup pecans, toasted

1 For dressing, whisk apple juice concentrate, vinegar, lemon juice, sugar, garlic, salt, onion powder and ginger in small bowl until blended. Slowly whisk in oil in thin, steady stream until well blended.

2 For salad, divide greens among four serving bowls. Top with chicken, tomatoes, apple chips, onion, cheese and pecans.

3 Drizzle about 2 tablespoons dressing over each salad.

SANDWICHES

CHICKEN PESTO FLATBREADS
MAKES 2 SERVINGS

2 (6- to 7-inch) round flatbreads or Greek-style pita bread rounds (no pocket)

2 tablespoons pesto

1 cup grilled chicken strips

4 slices mozzarella cheese

1 plum tomato, cut into ¼-inch slices

3 tablespoons shredded Parmesan cheese

1 Place flatbreads on work surface. Spread 1 tablespoon pesto over half of each flatbread. Place chicken on opposite half of bread; top with mozzarella, tomato and Parmesan. Fold pesto-topped bread half over filling.

2 Spray grill pan or nonstick skillet with nonstick cooking spray or brush with vegetable oil; heat over medium-high heat. Cook sandwiches about 3 minutes per side until bread is toasted, cheese begins to melt and sandwiches are heated through.

GUACAMOLE BURGERS

MAKES 4 SERVINGS

1 small avocado

2 tablespoons finely chopped tomato

1 tablespoon chopped fresh cilantro

2 teaspoons lime juice, divided

1 teaspoon minced jalapeño pepper*

¼ teaspoon salt, divided

2 tablespoons sour cream

2 tablespoons mayonnaise

½ teaspoon ground cumin

4 teaspoons vegetable oil, divided

1 medium onion, cut into thin slices

1 small green bell pepper, cut into thin slices

1 small red bell pepper, cut into thin slices

1¼ pounds ground beef

Salt and black pepper

4 slices Monterey Jack cheese

4 hamburger buns, split and toasted

1 can (4 ounces) diced fire-roasted jalapeño peppers, drained

Jalapeño peppers can sting and irritate the skin, so wear rubber gloves when handling peppers and do not touch your eyes.

1 Mash avocado in medium bowl. Stir in tomato, cilantro, 1 teaspoon lime juice, minced jalepeño and ⅛ teaspoon salt; mix well. Cover and refrigerate until ready to use. Combine sour cream, mayonnaise, remaining 1 teaspoon lime juice and cumin in small bowl; mix well. Cover and refrigerate until ready to use.

2 Heat 2 teaspoons oil in large skillet over medium-high heat. Add onion; cook about 8 minutes or until onion is very tender and begins to turn golden, stirring occasionally. (Add a few teaspoons water to skillet if onion begins to burn.) Remove to bowl. Add remaining 2 teaspoons oil to skillet. Add bell peppers; cook and stir 5 minutes or until tender. Remove to bowl with onion; season vegetables with remaining ⅛ teaspoon salt.

3 Preheat grill or broiler. Shape beef into four 5-inch patties; sprinkle both sides generously with salt and black pepper. Grill or broil patties about 5 minutes per side or until cooked through (160°F). Top patties with cheese slices during last minute of cooking.

4 Spread sour cream mixture over bottom halves of buns. Top with vegetables, burgers, guacamole, fire-roasted jalapeños and top halves of buns.

ALMOND CHICKEN SALAD SANDWICH

MAKES 4 SERVINGS

¼ cup mayonnaise

¼ cup plain Greek yogurt
or sour cream

2 tablespoons cider vinegar

1 tablespoon honey

1 teaspoon salt

½ teaspoon black pepper

⅛ teaspoon garlic powder

2 cups chopped cooked chicken

¾ cup halved red grapes

1 large stalk celery, chopped

⅓ cup sliced almonds

Leaf lettuce

1 tomato, thinly sliced

8 slices sesame semolina or
country Italian bread

1 Whisk mayonnaise, yogurt, vinegar, honey, salt, pepper and garlic powder in small bowl until well blended.

2 Combine chicken, grapes and celery in medium bowl. Add dressing; toss gently to coat. Cover and refrigerate several hours or overnight. Stir in almonds just before making sandwiches.

3 Place lettuce and tomato slices on four bread slices; top with chicken salad and remaining bread slices. Serve immediately.

TURKEY MOZZARELLA PANINI

MAKES 2 TO 4 SERVINGS

BACON JAM

- 1 pound thick-cut bacon, chopped
- 2 large onions, chopped (about 1 pound)
- ⅓ cup packed brown sugar
- ⅛ teaspoon red pepper flakes
- ⅔ cup water
- ¼ cup coffee
- 1½ tablespoons balsamic vinegar

GARLIC AIOLI

- ¼ cup mayonnaise
- 1 clove garlic, minced
- 1 teaspoon lemon juice
- ⅛ teaspoon salt

PANINI

- 2 (6- to 7-inch) round focaccia breads, split
- 2 plum tomatoes, cut into ¼-inch slices
- 6 ounces sliced fresh mozzarella (¼-inch-thick slices)
- 6 ounces thickly sliced turkey breast (about ¼-inch-thick slices)
- ½ cup baby arugula

1 For bacon jam, cook bacon in large skillet over medium-high heat 10 to 15 minutes or until bacon is cooked through but still chewy (not crisp), stirring occasionally. Remove bacon to paper towel-lined plate. Drain off all but 1 tablespoon drippings from skillet.

2 Add onions to skillet; cook 10 minutes, stirring occasionally. Add brown sugar and red pepper flakes; cook over medium-low heat 18 to 20 minutes or until onions are deep golden brown. Stir in bacon, water and coffee; cook over medium heat 25 minutes or until mixture is thick and jammy, stirring occasionally.* Stir in vinegar.

3 For garlic aioli, combine mayonnaise, garlic, lemon juice and salt in small bowl; mix well.

4 Spread bottom halves of focaccia with garlic aioli. Top with tomatoes, cheese, turkey and arugula. Spread top halves of focaccia with bacon jam; place over arugula. Cut sandwiches in half to serve.

Recipe makes about 1½ cups bacon jam. Store remaining jam in refrigerator up to 2 weeks; return to room temperature before serving.

SANDWICHES

NEW ORLEANS-STYLE MUFFALETTA

MAKES 4 TO 6 SERVINGS

¾ cup pitted green olives

½ cup pitted kalamata olives

½ cup giardiniera (Italian-style pickled vegetables), drained

2 tablespoons fresh parsley leaves

2 tablespoons capers

1 clove garlic, minced

2 tablespoons olive oil

1 tablespoon red wine vinegar

1 (8-inch) short round Italian loaf (16 to 22 ounces)

8 ounces thinly sliced ham

8 ounces thinly sliced Genoa salami

6 ounces thinly sliced provolone cheese

1 Combine olives, giardiniera, parsley, capers and garlic in food processor; pulse until coarsely chopped and no large pieces remain. Transfer to small bowl; stir in oil and vinegar until well blended. Cover and refrigerate several hours or overnight to blend flavors.

2 Cut bread in half crosswise. Spread two thirds of olive salad over bottom half of bread; layer with ham, salami and cheese. Spread remaining olive salad over cheese; top with top half of bread, pressing down slightly to compress. Wrap sandwich in plastic wrap; let stand 1 hour to blend flavors.

3 To serve sandwich warm, preheat oven to 350°F. Remove plastic wrap; wrap sandwich loosely in foil. Bake 5 to 10 minutes or just until sandwich is slightly warm and cheese begins to melt. Cut into wedges.

SANDWICHES

CHICKEN AND AVOCADO OVERSTUFFED QUESADILLAS

MAKES 2 SERVINGS

3 tablespoons Caesar dressing

2 teaspoons finely chopped fresh cilantro

2 burrito-size flour tortillas (10 to 11 inches)

¾ cup (3 ounces) shredded Monterey Jack cheese

1 cup chopped grilled chicken strips (¾-inch pieces)

½ cup shredded green cabbage

½ cup pico de gallo

1 avocado, sliced

2 tablespoons vegetable oil, divided

1 Combine dressing and cilantro in small bowl; mix well. Roll up tortillas in paper towel or waxed paper; microwave on HIGH 10 seconds or until softened.

2 Place tortillas on work surface. For each quesadilla, sprinkle ¼ cup cheese in circle in center of tortilla, leaving 3-inch border all around. Top with half of chicken; drizzle with half of dressing mixture. Top with half each of cabbage, pico de gallo and avocado; sprinkle with 2 tablespoons cheese.

3 Working with one tortilla at a time, fold top of tortilla down over filling to center. Hold folded part down while working in clockwise direction, folding down next section of tortilla to center until filling is completely covered. (You should end up with five folds and a hexagonal shape. If there is an uncovered hole in center of tortilla after folding, cut round piece from another tortilla to cover it.)

4 Heat 1 tablespoon oil in medium nonstick skillet over medium heat. Cook quesadilla, folded side down, about 5 minutes or until golden brown, pressing down with spatula. Turn and cook 4 to 5 minutes or until golden brown. Repeat with remaining 1 tablespoon oil and quesadilla.

HEARTY VEGGIE SANDWICH

MAKES 4 SERVINGS

1 pound cremini mushrooms, stemmed and thinly sliced (⅛-inch slices)

2 tablespoons olive oil, divided

¾ teaspoon salt, divided

¼ teaspoon black pepper

1 medium zucchini, diced (¼-inch pieces, about 2 cups)

3 tablespoons butter, softened

8 slices artisan whole grain bread

¼ cup prepared pesto

¼ cup mayonnaise

2 cups packed baby spinach

4 slices mozzarella cheese

1 Preheat oven to 350°F. Combine mushrooms, 1 tablespoon oil, ½ teaspoon salt and pepper in medium bowl; toss to coat. Spread on large rimmed baking sheet. Roast 20 minutes or until mushrooms are dark brown and dry, stirring after 10 minutes. Cool on baking sheet.

2 Meanwhile, heat remaining 1 tablespoon oil in large skillet over medium heat. Add zucchini and remaining ¼ teaspoon salt; cook and stir 5 minutes or until zucchini is tender and lightly browned. Transfer to bowl; wipe out skillet with paper towels.

3 Spread butter over one side of each bread slice. Turn over slices. Spread pesto over four slices; spread mayonnaise over remaining four slices. Top pesto-covered slices evenly with mushrooms, then spinach, zucchini and cheese. Top with remaining bread slices, mayonnaise side down.

4 Heat same skillet over medium heat. Add sandwiches; cover and cook 2 minutes per side or until bread is toasted, spinach is slightly wilted and cheese is beginning to melt. Cut sandwiches in half; serve immediately.

SANDWICHES

CHICKEN FAJITA ROLL-UPS

MAKES 4 SERVINGS

1 cup ranch dressing

1 teaspoon chili powder

2 tablespoons vegetable oil, divided

2 teaspoons lime juice

2 teaspoons fajita seasoning mix

½ teaspoon chipotle chili powder

¼ teaspoon salt

4 boneless skinless chicken breasts (about 6 ounces each)

4 fajita-size flour tortillas (8 to 9 inches)

1 cup (4 ounces) shredded Cheddar cheese

1 cup (4 ounces) shredded Monterey Jack cheese

3 cups shredded lettuce

1 cup pico de gallo

1 Combine ranch dressing and chili powder in small bowl; mix well. Refrigerate until ready to serve.

2 Combine 1 tablespoon oil, lime juice, fajita seasoning mix, chipotle chili powder and salt in small bowl; mix well. Coat both sides of chicken with spice mixture.

3 Heat remaining 1 tablespoon oil in large nonstick skillet or grill pan over medium-high heat. Add chicken; cook about 5 minutes per side or until cooked through. Remove to plate; let stand 5 minutes before slicing. Cut chicken breasts in half lengthwise, then cut crosswise into ½-inch strips.

4 Wipe out skillet with paper towel. Place one tortilla in skillet; sprinkle with ¼ cup Cheddar and ¼ cup Monterey Jack. Heat over medium heat until cheeses are melted. Remove tortilla to clean work surface or cutting board.

5 Sprinkle ¾ cup shredded lettuce down center of one tortilla; top with ¼ cup pico de gallo and one fourth of chicken. Fold bottom of tortilla up over filling, then fold in sides and roll up. Cut in half diagonally. Repeat with remaining tortillas, cheese and fillings. Serve with ranch dipping sauce.

SANDWICHES

CLASSIC PATTY MELTS
MAKES 4 SERVINGS

5 tablespoons butter, divided

2 large yellow onions, thinly sliced

¾ teaspoon plus pinch salt, divided

1 pound ground chuck (80% lean)

½ teaspoon garlic powder

½ teaspoon onion powder

¼ teaspoon black pepper

8 slices marble rye bread

½ cup Thousand Island dressing

8 slices deli American or Swiss cheese

1 Melt 2 tablespoons butter in large skillet over medium heat. Add onions and pinch of salt; cook 20 minutes or until onions are very soft and golden brown, stirring occasionally. Remove to small bowl; wipe out skillet with paper towel.

2 Combine beef, remaining ¾ teaspoon salt, garlic powder, onion powder and pepper in medium bowl; mix gently. Shape into four patties about the size and shape of bread slices and ¼ to ½ inch thick.

3 Melt 1 tablespoon butter in same skillet over medium-high heat. Add patties, two at a time; cook 3 minutes or until bottoms are browned, pressing down gently to form crust. Turn patties; cook 3 minutes or until browned. Remove patties to plate; wipe out skillet with paper towel.

4 Spread one side of each bread slice with dressing. Top four bread slices with cheese slice, patty, caramelized onions, another cheese slice and remaining bread slices.

5 Melt 1 tablespoon butter in same skillet over medium heat. Add two sandwiches to skillet; cook 4 minutes or until golden brown, pressing down to crisp bread. Turn sandwiches; cook 4 minutes or until golden brown and cheese is melted. Repeat with remaining 1 tablespoon butter and remaining sandwiches.

SOUTHWEST TURKEY SANDWICH
MAKES 4 SERVINGS

½ cup mayonnaise

1 tablespoon minced chipotle pepper in adobo sauce

1½ teaspoons lime juice

1 round loaf (16 ounces) cheese focaccia or cheese bread (preferably Asiago cheese)

1½ cups mixed greens

12 ounces sliced smoked turkey

½ red onion, thinly sliced

1 Combine mayonnaise, chipotle pepper and lime juice in small bowl; mix well.

2 Cut loaf in half horizontally; spread cut sides of bread with mayonnaise mixture. Top bottom half of loaf with mixed greens, turkey, onion and top half of bread. Cut into wedges.

MAIN DISHES

JAMBALAYA PASTA

MAKES 4 SERVINGS

1 pound boneless skinless chicken breasts, cut into 1-inch pieces

2 tablespoons plus 1 teaspoon Cajun spice blend, divided

1 tablespoon vegetable oil

8 ounces bell peppers (red, yellow, green or a combination), cut into ¼-inch strips

½ medium red onion, cut into ¼-inch strips

6 ounces medium raw shrimp, peeled and deveined

2 cloves garlic, minced

1 teaspoon salt

¼ teaspoon black pepper

1½ pounds plum tomatoes (about 6), cut into ½-inch pieces

1 cup chicken broth

1 package (16 ounces) fresh or dried linguini, cooked and drained

Chopped fresh parsley

1 Combine chicken and 2 tablespoons Cajun seasoning in medium bowl; toss to coat. Heat oil in large skillet over medium-high heat. Add chicken; cook and stir 3 minutes.

2 Add bell peppers and onion; cook and stir 3 minutes. Add shrimp, garlic, remaining 1 teaspoon Cajun seasoning, salt and black pepper; cook and stir 1 minute.

3 Stir in tomatoes and broth; bring to a boil. Reduce heat to medium-low; cook 3 minutes or until shrimp are pink and opaque. Serve over hot pasta; sprinkle with parsley.

STEAK FAJITAS

MAKES 2 SERVINGS

¼ cup lime juice

¼ cup soy sauce

4 tablespoons vegetable oil, divided

2 tablespoons honey

2 tablespoons Worcestershire sauce

2 cloves garlic, minced

½ teaspoon ground red pepper

1 pound flank steak, skirt steak or top sirloin

1 medium yellow onion, halved and cut into ¼-inch slices

1 green bell pepper, cut into ¼-inch strips

1 red bell pepper, cut into ¼-inch strips

Flour tortillas, warmed

Lime wedges (optional)

Optional toppings: pico de gallo, guacamole, sour cream, shredded lettuce and shredded Cheddar-Jack cheese

1 Combine lime juice, soy sauce, 2 tablespoons oil, honey, Worcestershire sauce, garlic and ground red pepper in medium bowl; mix well. Remove ¼ cup marinade to large bowl. Place steak in large resealable food storage bag. Pour remaining marinade over steak; seal bag and turn to coat. Marinate in refrigerator at least 2 hours or overnight. Add onion and bell peppers to bowl with ¼ cup marinade; toss to coat. Cover and refrigerate until ready to use.

2 Remove steak from marinade; discard marinade and wipe off excess from steak. Heat 1 tablespoon oil in large skillet (preferably cast iron) over medium-high heat. Cook steak about 4 minutes per side for medium rare or to desired doneness. Remove to cutting board; tent with foil and let stand 10 minutes.

3 Meanwhile, heat remaining 1 tablespoon oil in same skillet over medium-high heat. Add vegetable mixture; cook about 8 minutes or until vegetables are crisp-tender and beginning to brown in spots, stirring occasionally. (Cook in two batches if necessary; do not crowd vegetables in skillet.)

4 Cut steak into thin slices across the grain. Serve with vegetables, tortillas, lime wedges and desired toppings.

EGGPLANT PARMESAN
MAKES 4 SERVINGS

2 tablespoons olive oil

2 cloves garlic, minced

1 can (28 ounces) Italian whole tomatoes, undrained

½ cup water

1¼ teaspoons salt, divided

¼ teaspoon dried oregano

Pinch red pepper flakes

1 medium eggplant (about 1 pound)

⅓ cup all-purpose flour

Black pepper

⅔ cup milk

1 egg

1 cup Italian-seasoned dry bread crumbs

4 to 5 tablespoons vegetable oil, divided

1 cup (4 ounces) shredded mozzarella cheese

Chopped fresh parsley (optional)

1 Heat olive oil in medium saucepan over medium heat. Add garlic; cook and stir 2 minutes or until softened (do not brown). Crush tomatoes with hands (in bowl or in can); add to saucepan with juices from can. Stir in water, 1 teaspoon salt, oregano and red pepper flakes; bring to a simmer. Reduce heat to medium-low; cook 45 minutes, stirring occasionally.

2 Meanwhile, prepare eggplant. Cut eggplant crosswise into ¼-inch slices. Combine flour, remaining ¼ teaspoon salt and black pepper in shallow dish. Beat milk and egg in another shallow dish. Place bread crumbs in third shallow dish.

3 Coat both sides of eggplant slices with flour mixture, shaking off excess. Dip in egg mixture, letting excess drip back into dish. Roll in bread crumbs to coat.

4 Heat 3 tablespoons vegetable oil in large skillet over medium-high heat. Working in batches, add eggplant slices to skillet in single layer; cook 3 to 4 minutes per side or until golden brown, adding additional vegetable oil as needed. Remove to paper towel-lined plate; cover loosely with foil to keep warm.

5 Preheat broiler. Spray 13×9-inch baking dish with nonstick cooking spray. Arrange eggplant slices overlapping in baking dish; top with half of warm marinara sauce. (Reserve remaining marinara sauce for pasta or another use.) Sprinkle with cheese.

6 Broil 2 to 3 minutes or just until cheese is melted and beginning to brown. Garnish with parsley.

LEMON BUTTER CHICKEN

MAKES 4 SERVINGS

- 4 boneless skinless chicken breasts (about 6 ounces each)
- ½ teaspoon salt
- ¼ teaspoon black pepper
- 1 tablespoon olive oil
- 6 tablespoons (¾ stick) butter, divided
- ¼ cup finely chopped onion
- 2 cloves garlic, minced

- ½ cup dry white wine
- ¼ cup lemon juice
- 3 tablespoons thinly sliced oil-packed sun-dried tomatoes (about 4)
- 3 tablespoons slivered fresh basil, plus additional for garnish
- 1 package (4 ounces) goat cheese, cut into 4 pieces

1 Use meat mallet or rolling pin to pound chicken to ½-inch thickness between two sheets of plastic wrap. (Chicken may not need much flattening but make sure they are even thickness.) Season with salt and pepper.

2 Heat oil in large skillet over medium-high heat. Add chicken; cook 6 to 8 minutes per side or until lightly browned and no longer pink. Remove to plate; tent with foil to keep warm.

3 Add 1 tablespoon butter and onion to skillet; cook and stir 2 minutes or until softened. Add garlic; cook and stir 1 minute. Add wine and lemon juice; bring to a simmer. Cook about 10 minutes or until reduced by half.

4 Add remaining 5 tablespoons butter, 1 tablespoon at a time, whisking until smooth. Stir in sun-dried tomatoes and 3 tablespoons basil; cook just until heated through.

5 Place chicken on serving plates; top with goat cheese and sauce. Garnish with additional basil.

PARMESAN-CRUSTED TILAPIA

MAKES 4 SERVINGS

⅔ cup plus 3 tablespoons grated Parmesan cheese, divided

⅔ cup panko bread crumbs

⅓ cup prepared Alfredo sauce (refrigerated or jarred)

1½ teaspoons dried parsley flakes

4 tilapia fillets (6 ounces each)

Shaved Parmesan cheese (optional)

Minced fresh parsley (optional)

1 Preheat oven to 425°F. Line baking sheet with foil; spray foil with nonstick cooking spray.

2 Combine ⅔ cup grated cheese and panko in medium bowl; mix well. Combine Alfredo sauce, remaining 3 tablespoons grated cheese and parsley flakes in small bowl; mix well.

3 Spread sauce mixture over top of fish fillets, coating in thick, even layer. Top with panko mixture, pressing in gently to adhere. Place fish on prepared baking sheet.

4 Bake on top rack of oven about 15 minutes or until crust is golden brown and fish begins to flake when tested with fork. Garnish with shaved Parmesan and fresh parsley.

CLASSIC LASAGNA

MAKES 6 TO 8 SERVINGS

1 tablespoon olive oil

8 ounces bulk mild Italian sausage

8 ounces ground beef

1 medium onion, chopped

3 cloves garlic, minced, divided

1½ teaspoons salt, divided

1 can (28 ounces) crushed tomatoes

1 can (28 ounces) diced tomatoes

2 teaspoons Italian seasoning

1 egg

1 container (15 ounces) ricotta cheese

¾ cup grated Parmesan cheese, divided

½ cup minced fresh parsley

¼ teaspoon black pepper

12 uncooked no-boil lasagna noodles

4 cups (16 ounces) shredded mozzarella

1 Preheat oven to 350°F. Spray 13×9-inch baking dish with nonstick cooking spray.

2 Heat oil in large saucepan over medium-high heat. Add sausage, beef, onion, 2 cloves garlic and 1 teaspoon salt; cook and stir 10 minutes or until meat is no longer pink, breaking up meat with wooden spoon. Add crushed tomatoes, diced tomatoes and Italian seasoning; bring to a boil. Reduce heat to medium-low; cook 15 minutes, stirring occasionally.

3 Meanwhile, beat egg in medium bowl. Stir in ricotta, ½ cup Parmesan, parsley, remaining 1 clove garlic, ½ teaspoon salt and pepper until well blended.

4 Spread ¼ cup sauce in prepared baking dish. Top with 3 noodles, breaking to fit if necessary. Spread one third of ricotta mixture over noodles. Sprinkle with 1 cup mozzarella; top with 2 cups sauce. Repeat layers of noodles, ricotta mixture, mozzarella and sauce two times. Top with remaining 3 noodles, sauce, 1 cup mozzarella and ¼ cup Parmesan. Cover dish with foil sprayed with cooking spray.

5 Bake 30 minutes. Remove foil; bake 10 to 15 minutes or until hot and bubbly. Let stand 10 minutes before serving.

MAIN DISHES

MONGOLIAN BEEF
MAKES 4 SERVINGS

1¼ pounds beef flank steak

¼ cup cornstarch

3 tablespoons vegetable oil, divided

3 cloves garlic, minced

2 teaspoons grated fresh ginger

½ cup water

½ cup soy sauce

⅓ cup packed dark brown sugar

Pinch red pepper flakes

2 green onions, diagonally sliced into 1-inch pieces

Hot cooked rice (optional)

1 Cut flank steak in half lengthwise, then cut crosswise (against the grain) into ¼-inch slices. Combine beef and cornstarch in medium bowl; toss to coat.

2 Heat 1 tablespoon oil in large skillet or wok over high heat. Add half of beef in single layer (do not crowd); cook 1 to 2 minutes per side or until browned. Remove to clean bowl. Repeat with remaining beef and 1 tablespoon oil.

3 Heat remaining 1 tablespoon oil in same skillet over medium heat. Add garlic and ginger; cook and stir 30 seconds. Add water, soy sauce, brown sugar and red pepper flakes; bring to a boil, stirring until well blended. Cook about 8 minutes or until slightly thickened.

4 Return beef to skillet; cook 2 to 3 minutes or until sauce thickens and beef is heated through. Stir in green onions. Serve over rice, if desired.

MISO SALMON

MAKES 4 SERVINGS

1 cup uncooked long grain rice

4 salmon fillets (about 6 ounces each)

¼ cup packed brown sugar

¼ cup red or white miso

2 tablespoons soy sauce

1 tablespoon hot water

1 tablespoon butter

1 tablespoon minced fresh ginger

1 tablespoon minced shallot or red onion

½ cup plus 1 teaspoon sake, divided

1 tablespoon whipping cream or half-and-half

½ cup (1 stick) cold butter, cut into small pieces

1 teaspoon lime juice

½ teaspoon salt

2 green onions, cut into julienne strips

1 Cook rice according to package directions; keep warm.

2 Preheat broiler. Spray 13×9-inch baking pan with nonstick cooking spray. Place salmon in prepared pan.

3 Whisk brown sugar, miso, soy sauce and hot water in small bowl until well blended. Spoon half of mixture evenly over fish. Broil 10 minutes or until fish begins to flake when tested with fork, spooning remaining mixture over fish twice during cooking.

4 Meanwhile, melt 1 tablespoon butter in small saucepan over medium heat. Add ginger and shallot; cook and stir 3 minutes or until softened. Add ½ cup sake; bring to a boil over medium-high heat. Cook 3 to 5 minutes or until reduced to 2 tablespoons. Whisk in cream. Add cold butter, one piece at a time, whisking constantly until butter is incorporated before adding next piece. Remove from heat; whisk in remaining 1 teaspoon sake, lime juice and ½ teaspoon salt. Season with additional salt, if desired.

5 Spread sauce on four plates; top with rice, fish and green onions.

LITTLE ITALY BAKED ZITI

MAKES 6 TO 8 SERVINGS

1 package (16 ounces) uncooked ziti pasta

1 pound bulk mild Italian sausage

3 cloves garlic, minced

¾ cup dry white wine

1 jar (24 ounces) marinara sauce

1 can (about 14 ounces) diced tomatoes

2 tablespoons butter

2 cups (8 ounces) shredded mozzarella cheese, divided

½ cup coarsely chopped fresh basil, plus additional for garnish

¼ cup grated Parmesan cheese

1 Cook pasta in large saucepan of boiling salted water until al dente. Drain and return to saucepan; keep warm.

2 Meanwhile, cook sausage in large skillet over medium-high heat about 8 minutes or until no longer pink, stirring to break up meat. Add garlic; cook and stir 1 minute. Add wine; cook about 4 minutes or until almost evaporated.

3 Stir in marinara sauce, tomatoes and butter; bring to a boil. Reduce heat to medium-low; cook 20 minutes, stirring occasionally. Preheat broiler. Spray 3-quart or 13×9-inch broilerproof baking dish with nonstick cooking spray.

4 Add sauce mixture, 1 cup mozzarella and ½ cup basil to pasta in saucepan; stir gently to coat. Spread in prepared baking dish; sprinkle with remaining 1 cup mozzarella and Parmesan.

5 Broil 2 to 3 minutes or until cheese begins to bubble and turn golden brown. Garnish with additional basil.

RESTAURANT-STYLE BABY BACK RIBS

MAKES 4 SERVINGS

1¼ cups water

1 cup white vinegar

⅔ cup packed dark brown sugar

½ cup tomato paste

1 tablespoon yellow mustard

1½ teaspoons salt

1 teaspoon liquid smoke

1 teaspoon onion powder

½ teaspoon garlic powder

½ teaspoon paprika

2 racks pork baby back ribs (3½ to 4 pounds total)

1 Combine water, vinegar, brown sugar, tomato paste, mustard, salt, liquid smoke, onion powder, garlic powder and paprika in medium saucepan; bring to a boil over medium heat. Reduce heat to medium-low; cook 40 minutes or until sauce thickens, stirring occasionally.

2 Preheat oven to 300°F. Place each rack of ribs on large sheet of heavy-duty foil. Brush some of sauce over ribs, covering completely. Fold down edges of foil tightly to seal and create packet; arrange packets on baking sheet, seam sides up.

3 Bake 2 hours. Prepare grill or preheat broiler. Carefully open packets and drain off excess liquid.

4 Brush ribs with sauce; grill or broil about 5 minutes per side or until beginning to char, brushing with sauce once or twice during grilling. Serve with remaining sauce.

MAIN DISHES

BANGKOK PEANUT NOODLES
MAKES 4 SERVINGS

SAUCE

- 6 tablespoons peanut butter
- ¼ cup soy sauce
- 1 tablespoon unseasoned rice vinegar
- 1 tablespoon packed brown sugar
- 1 tablespoon sriracha sauce
- 2 teaspoons grated fresh ginger
- 2 cloves garlic, minced
- 2 teaspoons dark sesame oil

STIR-FRY

- 1 package (6 ounces) dried chow mein stir-fry noodles
- 1 pound boneless skinless chicken breasts, cut into 1-inch pieces *or* 1 package (14 ounces) extra firm tofu, cut into ½-inch cubes
- ½ cup cornstarch
- 3 tablespoons vegetable oil, divided
- 1 red bell pepper, cut into thin strips
- ½ medium onion, thinly sliced
- 2 cups sliced Swiss chard or bok choy

1 For sauce, whisk peanut butter, soy sauce, vinegar, brown sugar, sriracha, ginger, garlic and sesame oil in small bowl until smooth.

2 For stir-fry, cook noodles according to package directions; drain and rinse under cold water until cool.

3 Combine chicken and cornstarch in medium bowl; toss to coat. Heat 2 tablespoons vegetable oil in large skillet over medium-high heat. Add chicken; stir-fry 5 minutes or until chicken is golden brown and cooked through. Drain on paper towel-lined plate. Wipe out skillet with paper towel.

4 Heat remaining 1 tablespoon vegetable oil in same skillet over high heat. Add bell pepper and onion; stir-fry 5 minutes or until browned. Add chard; stir-fry 1 minute or until wilted. Add noodles and sauce; cook until noodles are coated with sauce. Add 1 tablespoon water if needed to loosen sauce. Return chicken to skillet; stir to coat. Cook just until heated through.

CHICKEN MADEIRA

MAKES 4 SERVINGS

- 4 boneless skinless chicken breasts (about 6 ounces each)
- ½ teaspoon salt
- ¼ teaspoon black pepper
- 3 tablespoons butter, divided
- 1 tablespoon olive oil
- 8 ounces mushrooms, sliced
- 1½ cups Madeira wine
- 1½ cups beef broth
- 8 ounces fresh asparagus, trimmed
- ¼ cup plus 1 tablespoon water, divided
- 1 tablespoon cornstarch
- 4 slices mozzarella cheese

1 Use meat mallet or rolling pin to pound chicken to ¼-inch thickness between two pieces of plastic wrap. Season with salt and pepper.

2 Heat 1 tablespoon butter and oil in large skillet over medium heat. Add chicken; cook 4 to 5 minutes per side or until lightly browned and no longer pink in center. Remove to plate; tent with foil. Add 1 tablespoon butter and mushrooms to skillet; cook about 8 minutes or until mushrooms are browned and liquid has evaporated, stirring occasionally and scraping up browned bits from bottom of skillet. Remove mushrooms to medium bowl.

3 Add Madeira and broth to skillet; bring to a boil over high heat. Reduce heat to medium; cook 10 to 12 minutes or until sauce is reduced by half. Meanwhile, preheat broiler. Place asparagus in medium microwavable dish with ¼ cup water; cover with vented plastic wrap. Microwave on HIGH 4 minutes or until crisp-tender.

4 Stir remaining 1 tablespoon water into cornstarch in small bowl until smooth. Whisk into reduced sauce in skillet; cook and stir 2 minutes or until thickened. Add remaining 1 tablespoon butter; stir until melted. Stir in cooked mushrooms.

5 Place chicken on baking sheet; top with cheese and asparagus. Broil 2 minutes or until cheese is melted. Transfer chicken to serving plates; top with sauce.

MAIN DISHES

RENEGADE STEAK

MAKES 2 SERVINGS

1½ teaspoons coarse salt
½ teaspoon paprika
½ teaspoon black pepper
¼ teaspoon onion powder
¼ teaspoon garlic powder
⅛ teaspoon ground turmeric

⅛ teaspoon ground red pepper
⅛ teaspoon ground coriander
2 center-cut sirloin or strip steaks (about 8 ounces each)
2 tablespoons vegetable oil
1 tablespoon butter

1 Combine salt, paprika, black pepper, onion powder, garlic powder, turmeric, red pepper and coriander in small bowl; mix well. Season both sides of steaks with spice mixture (you will not need all of it); let steaks stand at room temperature 45 minutes before cooking.

2 Heat large cast iron skillet over high heat. Add oil; heat until oil shimmers and just begins to smoke. Add steaks to skillet; cook 30 seconds, then turn steaks. Cook 30 seconds, then turn again. Continue cooking and turning every 30 seconds for about 4 minutes or until golden brown crust begins to form.

3 Add butter; continue cooking and turning every 30 seconds for about 1 minute or until steaks reach 130° to 135°F for medium rare or 140° to 145°F for medium.* Remove to plate; let steaks rest 5 minutes before serving.

Timing given is approximate for 1½-inch steaks; thinner steaks will take less time to cook.

MAIN DISHES

CHICKEN BOWTIE PARTY

MAKES 4 SERVINGS

1 package (10 to 12 ounces) uncooked bowtie pasta

6 slices bacon, chopped

12 ounces boneless skinless chicken breasts, cut into 2×½-inch strips*

⅓ cup chopped red onion

1 teaspoon minced garlic

2 plum tomatoes, diced (about ½ cup)

1 cup whipping cream

¼ cup shredded Asiago cheese, plus additional for garnish

1 jar (15 ounces) Alfredo sauce

Finely chopped fresh parsley (optional)

Or substitute 12 ounces grilled chicken breast strips; add to skillet with tomatoes in step 3.

1 Cook pasta in large saucepan of salted boiling water until al dente. Drain and return to saucepan; keep warm.

2 Meanwhile, cook bacon in large skillet over medium-high heat until cooked through. (Bacon should still be chewy, not quite crisp.) Remove to paper towel-lined plate. Drain all but 1 tablespoon drippings from skillet.

3 Add chicken to skillet; cook about 4 minutes or until chicken begins to brown, turning occasionally. Add onion and garlic; cook and stir 2 minutes. Add tomatoes and bacon; cook and stir 1 minute. Stir in cream and ¼ cup cheese; cook about 4 minutes or until liquid is slightly reduced.

4 Add chicken mixture and Alfredo sauce to pasta in saucepan; stir gently to coat. Cook over medium heat until heated through, stirring occasionally. Garnish with parsley and additional cheese.

DOUBLE DECKER TACOS
MAKES 8 TACOS

2 tablespoons all-purpose flour
2 teaspoons chili powder
1 teaspoon dried minced onion
¾ teaspoon paprika
½ teaspoon salt
½ teaspoon garlic powder
¼ teaspoon sugar
1 pound ground beef
⅔ cup water
8 taco shells

8 mini (5-inch) flour tortillas*
2 cups refried beans, warmed
2 cups shredded romaine
    lettuce
1 cup chopped tomato
1 cup (4 ounces) shredded
    Cheddar cheese
Sour cream (optional)

Mini flour tortillas may also be labeled as street tacos.

1 Preheat oven to 350°F. Combine flour, chili powder, onion, paprika, salt, garlic powder and sugar in small bowl; mix well.

2 Cook beef in large skillet over medium-high heat until browned, stirring frequently to break up meat. Drain fat and excess liquid from skillet. Add flour mixture; cook and stir 2 minutes. Stir in water; bring to a simmer. Reduce heat to medium; cook about 10 minutes or until most of liquid has evaporated. Meanwhile, heat taco shells in oven about 5 minutes or until warm.

3 Wrap tortillas in damp paper towel; microwave on HIGH 25 to 35 seconds or until warm. Spread each tortilla with ¼ cup refried beans, leaving ¼-inch border around edge. Wrap flour tortillas around outside of taco shells, pressing gently to seal together.

4 Fill taco shells with beef mixture; top with lettuce, tomato and cheese. Drizzle with sour cream, if desired. Serve immediately.

SIDE DISHES

HEARTY HASH BROWN CASSEROLE

MAKES ABOUT 16 SERVINGS

2 cups sour cream

2 cups (8 ounces) shredded Colby cheese, divided

1 can (10¾ ounces) cream of chicken soup

½ cup (1 stick) butter, melted

1 small onion, finely chopped

¾ teaspoon salt

½ teaspoon black pepper

1 package (30 ounces) frozen shredded hash brown potatoes, thawed

1 Preheat oven to 375°F. Spray 13×9-inch baking dish with nonstick cooking spray.

2 Combine sour cream, 1½ cups cheese, soup, butter, onion, salt and pepper in large bowl; mix well. Add potatoes; stir until well blended. Spread mixture in prepared baking dish. (Do not pack down.) Sprinkle with remaining ½ cup cheese.

3 Bake about 45 minutes or until cheese is melted and top of casserole is beginning to brown.

STEAKHOUSE CREAMED SPINACH

MAKES 4 SERVINGS

1 pound baby spinach
½ cup (1 stick) butter
2 tablespoons finely chopped onion
¼ cup all-purpose flour
2 cups whole milk

1 bay leaf
½ teaspoon salt
Pinch ground nutmeg
Pinch ground red pepper
Black pepper

1 Heat medium saucepan of water to a boil over high heat. Add spinach; cook 1 minute. Drain and transfer to bowl of ice water to stop cooking. Squeeze spinach dry; coarsely chop. Wipe out saucepan with paper towel.

2 Melt butter in same saucepan over medium heat. Add onion; cook and stir 2 minutes or until softened. Add flour; cook and stir 2 to 3 minutes or until slightly golden. Slowly add milk in thin, steady stream, whisking constantly until mixture boils and begins to thicken. Stir in bay leaf, ½ teaspoon salt, nutmeg and red pepper. Reduce heat to low; cook 5 minutes, stirring frequently. Remove and discard bay leaf.

3 Stir in spinach; cook 5 minutes, stirring frequently. Season with additional salt and black pepper.

SIMPLE GOLDEN CORN BREAD

MAKES 9 TO 12 SERVINGS

1¼ cups all-purpose flour
¾ cup yellow cornmeal
⅓ cup sugar
2 teaspoons baking powder
1 teaspoon salt

1¼ cups whole milk
¼ cup (½ stick) butter, melted
1 egg
Honey Butter (recipe follows, optional)

1 Preheat oven to 400°F. Spray 8-inch square baking dish or pan with nonstick cooking spray.

2 Combine flour, cornmeal, sugar, baking powder and salt in large bowl; mix well. Beat milk, butter and egg in medium bowl until well blended. Add to flour mixture; stir just until dry ingredients are moistened. Pour batter into prepared baking dish.

3 Bake 25 minutes or until golden brown and toothpick inserted into center comes out clean. Prepare Honey Butter, if desired. Serve with corn bread.

HONEY BUTTER

Beat 6 tablespoons (¾ stick) softened butter and
¼ cup honey in medium bowl with electric mixer
at medium-high speed until light and creamy.

CLASSIC MACARONI AND CHEESE

MAKES 8 SERVINGS

2 cups uncooked elbow
   macaroni
¼ cup (½ stick) butter
¼ cup all-purpose flour
2½ cups whole milk

1 teaspoon salt
⅛ teaspoon black pepper
4 cups (16 ounces) shredded
   Colby-Jack cheese

1 Cook pasta according to package directions until al dente; drain.

2 Melt butter in large saucepan over medium heat. Add flour; whisk until well blended and bubbly. Gradually add milk, salt and pepper, whisking until blended. Cook and stir until milk begins to bubble. Add cheese, 1 cup at a time; cook and stir until cheese is melted and sauce is smooth.

3 Add cooked pasta to saucepan; stir gently until blended. Cook until heated through.

SIDE DISHES

CHICKEN FRIED RICE

MAKES 4 SERVINGS

2 tablespoons vegetable oil, divided

12 ounces boneless skinless chicken breasts, cut into ½-inch cubes

Salt and black pepper

2 tablespoons butter

2 cloves garlic, minced

½ sweet onion, diced

1 medium carrot, diced

2 green onions, thinly sliced

3 eggs

4 cups cooked rice*

3 tablespoons soy sauce

2 tablespoons sesame seeds

For rice, cook 1½ cups rice according to package directions without oil or butter. Spread hot rice on large rimmed baking sheet; cool to room temperature. Refrigerate several hours or overnight. Measure 4 cups.

1 Heat 1 tablespoon oil in large skillet over medium-high heat. Add chicken; season with salt and pepper. Cook and stir 5 to 6 minutes or until cooked through. Add butter and garlic; cook and stir 1 minute or until butter is melted. Remove to small bowl.

2 Add sweet onion, carrot and green onions to skillet; cook and stir over high heat 3 minutes or until vegetables are softened. Add to bowl with chicken.

3 Heat remaining 1 tablespoon oil in same skillet. Crack eggs into skillet; cook and stir 45 seconds or until eggs are scrambled but still moist. Add chicken and vegetable mixture, rice, soy sauce and sesame seeds; cook and stir 2 minutes or until well blended and heated through. Season with additional salt and pepper.

CHEDDAR BISCUITS

MAKES 15 BISCUITS

2 cups all-purpose flour

1 tablespoon sugar

1 tablespoon baking powder

2¼ teaspoons garlic powder, divided

¾ teaspoon plus pinch of salt, divided

1 cup whole milk

½ cup (1 stick) plus 3 tablespoons butter, melted, divided

2 cups (8 ounces) shredded Cheddar cheese

½ teaspoon dried parsley flakes

1 Preheat oven to 450°F. Line baking sheet with parchment paper.

2 Combine flour, sugar, baking powder, 2 teaspoons garlic powder and ¾ teaspoon salt in large bowl; mix well. Add milk and ½ cup butter; stir just until dry ingredients are moistened. Stir in cheese just until blended. Drop scant ¼ cupfuls of dough about 1½ inches apart onto prepared baking sheet.

3 Bake 10 to 12 minutes or until golden brown.

4 Meanwhile, combine remaining 3 tablespoons melted butter, ¼ teaspoon garlic powder, pinch of salt and parsley flakes in small bowl; brush over biscuits immediately after removing from oven. Serve warm.

LOADED BAKED POTATOES

MAKES 4 SERVINGS

4 large baking potatoes
1 cup (4 ounces) shredded Cheddar cheese
1 cup (4 ounces) shredded Monterey Jack cheese
8 slices bacon, crisp-cooked
½ cup sour cream

¼ cup (½ stick) butter, melted
2 tablespoons milk
1 teaspoon salt
¼ teaspoon black pepper
1 tablespoon vegetable oil
2 teaspoons coarse sea salt
1 green onion, thinly sliced

1 Preheat oven to 400°F. Poke potatoes all over with fork; place in small baking pan. Bake about 1 hour or until potatoes are fork-tender. Let stand until cool enough to handle. *Reduce oven temperature to 350°F.*

2 Combine Cheddar and Monterey Jack in small bowl; reserve ¼ cup for garnish. Chop bacon; reserve ¼ cup for garnish.

3 Cut off thin slice from one long side of each potato. Scoop out centers of potatoes, leaving ¼-inch shell. Place flesh from 3 potatoes in medium bowl. (Reserve flesh from fourth potato for another use.) Add sour cream, butter, remaining 1¾ cups shredded cheese, bacon, milk, 1 teaspoon salt and pepper to bowl with potatoes; mash until well blended.

4 Turn potato shells over; brush bottoms and sides with oil. Sprinkle evenly with sea salt. Turn right side up and return to baking pan. Fill shells with mashed potato mixture, mounding over tops of shells. Sprinkle with reserved cheese and bacon.

5 Bake about 20 minutes or until filling is hot and cheese is melted. Garnish with green onion.

CINNAMON APPLES

MAKES 4 SERVINGS

¼ cup (½ stick) butter

3 tart red apples such as Gala, Fuji or Honeycrisp (about 1½ pounds total), peeled and cut into ½-inch wedges

¼ cup packed brown sugar

1 teaspoon ground cinnamon

⅛ teaspoon ground nutmeg

⅛ teaspoon salt

1 tablespoon cornstarch

1 Melt butter in large skillet over medium-high heat. Add apples; cook about 8 minutes or until apples are tender, stirring occasionally.

2 Add brown sugar, cinnamon, nutmeg and salt; cook and stir 1 minute or until glazed. Reduce heat to medium-low; stir in cornstarch until well blended.

3 Remove from heat; let stand 5 minutes for glaze to thicken. Stir again; serve immediately.

PARMESAN ALFREDO PASTA BAKE

MAKES 6 TO 8 SERVINGS

2 tablespoons plus ½ teaspoon salt, divided

1 package (16 ounces) uncooked fusilli pasta

6 tablespoons (¾ stick) butter

1 clove garlic

1 cup whipping cream

1 cup milk

2 cups shredded Parmesan cheese, divided

1 cup (4 ounces) shredded mozzarella cheese

4 ounces mozzarella cheese, cubed

1 cup panko bread crumbs

2 tablespoons butter, melted

¼ teaspoon Italian seasoning

1 Preheat oven to 400°F. Spray 3-quart baking dish with nonstick cooking spray.

2 Bring large saucepan of water to a boil; stir in 2 tablespoons salt. Add pasta; cook according to package directions until al dente. Drain pasta, reserving ½ cup cooking water. Return pasta to saucepan.

3 Meanwhile, melt 6 tablespoons butter in medium saucepan over medium heat. Add garlic and remaining ½ teaspoon salt. Stir in cream, milk and ½ cup pasta water; bring to a simmer. Remove from heat; remove and discard garlic clove. Gradually stir in 1 cup Parmesan and shredded mozzarella until smooth and well blended. Pour over pasta; stir gently to coat. Pour into prepared baking dish; fold in cubed mozzarella.

4 Combine panko, remaining 1 cup Parmesan and 2 tablespoons melted butter in medium bowl. Spread evenly over pasta mixture; sprinkle with Italian seasoning.

5 Bake 15 minutes or until topping is golden brown and pasta is heated through.

HUSH PUPPIES

MAKES ABOUT 24 HUSH PUPPIES

1½ cups yellow cornmeal
½ cup all-purpose flour
2 teaspoons baking powder
¾ teaspoon salt
1 cup milk

1 small onion, minced
1 egg, lightly beaten
Vegetable oil
Ketchup (optional)

1 Combine cornmeal, flour, baking powder and salt in medium bowl; mix well. Add milk, onion and egg; stir until well blended. Let batter stand 5 to 10 minutes.

2 Heat 1 inch of oil in large heavy skillet over medium heat to 375°F; adjust heat to maintain temperature. Drop batter by tablespoonfuls into hot oil. Cook, in batches, 2 minutes or until golden brown. Drain on paper towel-lined plate. Serve warm with ketchup, if desired.

DESSERTS

KEY LIME PIE
MAKES 8 SERVINGS

12 whole graham crackers*
⅓ cup butter, melted
3 tablespoons sugar
2 cans (14 ounces each)
    sweetened condensed milk
¾ cup key lime juice

6 egg yolks
Pinch salt
Whipped cream (optional)
Lime slices (optional)

Or substitute 1½ cups graham cracker crumbs.

1 Preheat oven to 350°F. Spray 9-inch pie plate or springform pan with nonstick cooking spray.

2 Place graham crackers in food processor; pulse until coarse crumbs form. Add butter and sugar; pulse until well blended. Press mixture onto bottom and 1 inch up side of prepared pie plate. Bake 8 minutes or until lightly browned. Remove to wire rack to cool 10 minutes. *Reduce oven temperature to 325°F.*

3 Meanwhile, beat sweetened condensed milk, lime juice, egg yolks and salt in large bowl with electric mixer at medium-low speed 1 minute or until well blended and smooth. Pour into crust.

4 Bake 20 minutes or until top is set. Cool completely in pan on wire rack. Cover and refrigerate 2 hours or overnight. Garnish with whipped cream and lime slices.

BROWNIE LASAGNA

MAKES 6 TO 12 SERVINGS

BROWNIE

- ¾ cup unsweetened cocoa powder
- ¾ cup (1½ sticks) butter, melted
- 1⅓ cups all-purpose flour
- ½ teaspoon baking powder
- ½ teaspoon salt
- ½ teaspoon espresso powder or instant coffee granules
- 1⅔ cups granulated sugar
- 2 tablespoons vegetable oil
- 2 tablespoons water
- 3 eggs
- 1 teaspoon vanilla

FROSTING

- 1 package (8 ounces) cream cheese, softened
- ½ cup (1 stick) butter, softened
- 2½ cups powdered sugar
- 2 teaspoons vanilla
- Chocolate shavings (optional)
- Hot fudge topping or chocolate sauce, warmed

1 For brownie, preheat oven to 350°F. Line 13×9-inch baking pan with parchment paper or spray generously with nonstick cooking spray.

2 Stir cocoa into warm melted butter in large bowl until well blended and smooth; let stand 5 minutes. Combine flour, baking powder, salt and espresso powder in medium bowl; mix well. Add granulated sugar, oil and water to cocoa mixture; stir until well blended. Beat in eggs, one at a time, until blended. Stir in 1 teaspoon vanilla. Add flour mixture; stir until blended. Spread batter evenly in prepared pan.

3 Bake about 18 minutes or until toothpick inserted into center comes out with fudgy crumbs. Cool completely in pan on wire rack. Cover and refrigerate 4 hours or overnight (to make cutting easier).

4 For frosting, beat cream cheese and softened butter in large bowl with electric mixer at medium speed about 3 minutes or until creamy. Add powdered sugar and 2 teaspoons vanilla; beat at low speed until blended. Beat at medium speed 2 minutes or until smooth.

5 Remove brownie from pan; place on cutting board. Cut in half crosswise, then cut each piece in half horizontally with serrated knife to create total of four thin layers.

6 Place one brownie layer on serving plate; spread with ⅔ cup frosting. Repeat layers three times. Refrigerate at least 2 hours before serving. Top with chocolate shavings, if desired; drizzle with hot fudge topping.

RASPBERRY WHITE CHOCOLATE CHEESECAKE

MAKES 12 SERVINGS

24 crème-filled chocolate sandwich cookies, crushed into fine crumbs

3 tablespoons butter, melted

4 packages (8 ounces each) cream cheese, softened

1¼ cups sugar

½ cup sour cream

2 teaspoons vanilla

5 eggs, at room temperature

1 bar (4 ounces) white chocolate, chopped into ¼-inch pieces

¾ cup seedless raspberry jam, stirred

Shaved white chocolate

Whipped cream and fresh raspberries

1 Preheat oven to 350°F. Spray 9-inch springform pan with nonstick cooking spray. Line bottom and side of pan with parchment paper. Wrap outside of pan tightly with foil.

2 For crust, combine crushed cookies and butter in small bowl; mix well. Press mixture onto bottom and 1 inch up side of prepared pan. Bake about 8 minutes or until firm. Remove to wire rack to cool completely. *Increase oven temperature to 450°F.*

3 Beat cream cheese in large bowl with electric mixer at low speed until creamy. Add sugar, sour cream and vanilla; beat until smooth and well blended. Add eggs, one at a time, beating until blended after each addition. Fold in chopped white chocolate with spatula. Spread one third of filling in crust. Drop half of jam by teaspoonfuls over filling; swirl gently with small knife or skewer, being careful not to overmix. Top with one third of filling; drop remaining jam by teaspoonfuls over filling and gently swirl jam. Spread remaining filling over top.

4 Place springform pan in roasting pan; fill roasting pan with hot water to come halfway up side of springform pan. Carefully place in oven. *Immediately reduce oven temperature to 350°F.* Bake about 1 hour 10 minutes or until top of cheesecake is lightly browned and center jiggles slightly. Remove cheesecake from roasting pan to wire rack; remove foil. Cool to room temperature. Cover and refrigerate 4 hours or overnight. Top with shaved white chocolate, whipped cream and raspberries.

FRENCH SILK PIE

MAKES 8 SERVINGS

1 9-inch deep-dish pie crust (frozen or refrigerated)

1⅓ cups granulated sugar

¾ cup (1½ sticks) butter, softened

4 ounces unsweetened chocolate, melted

1½ tablespoons unsweetened cocoa powder

1 teaspoon vanilla

⅛ teaspoon salt

4 pasteurized eggs*

1 cup whipping cream

2 tablespoons powdered sugar

Chocolate curls (optional)

The eggs in this recipe are not cooked, so use pasteurized eggs to ensure food safety.

1 Bake pie crust according to package directions. Cool completely on wire rack.

2 Beat granulated sugar and butter in large bowl with electric mixer at medium speed about 4 minutes or until light and fluffy. Add melted chocolate, cocoa, vanilla and salt; beat until well blended. Add eggs, one at a time, beating 4 minutes after each addition and scraping down side of bowl occasionally.

3 Spread filling in cooled crust; refrigerate at least 3 hours or overnight.

4 Beat cream and powdered sugar in medium bowl with electric mixer at high speed until soft peaks form. Pipe or spread whipped cream over chocolate layer; garnish with chocolate curls.

CARROT CAKE
MAKES 8 TO 10 SERVINGS

CAKE

- 2 cups all-purpose flour
- 2 teaspoons baking soda
- 2 teaspoons ground cinnamon
- 1 teaspoon salt
- 4 eggs
- 2¼ cups granulated sugar
- 1 cup vegetable oil
- 1 cup buttermilk
- 1 tablespoon vanilla
- 3 medium carrots, shredded (3 cups)
- 3 cups walnuts, chopped and toasted, divided
- 1 cup shredded coconut
- 1 can (8 ounces) crushed pineapple

FROSTING

- 2 packages (8 ounces each) cream cheese, softened
- 1 cup (2 sticks) butter, softened
- Pinch salt
- 3 cups powdered sugar
- 1 tablespoon orange juice
- 2 teaspoons grated orange peel
- 1 teaspoon vanilla

1 Preheat oven to 350°F. Spray two 9-inch round cake pans with nonstick cooking spray. Line bottoms of pans with parchment paper; spray paper with cooking spray.

2 For cake, combine flour, baking soda, cinnamon and 1 teaspoon salt in medium bowl; mix well. Whisk eggs in large bowl until blended. Add granulated sugar, oil, buttermilk and 1 tablespoon vanilla; whisk until well blended. Add flour mixture; stir until well blended. Add carrots, 1 cup walnuts, coconut and pineapple; stir just until blended. Pour batter into prepared pans.

3 Bake 25 to 30 minutes or until toothpick inserted into centers comes out clean. Cool in pans 10 minutes; remove to wire racks to cool completely.

4 For frosting, beat cream cheese, butter and pinch of salt in large bowl with electric mixer at medium speed 3 minutes or until creamy. Add powdered sugar, orange juice, orange peel and 1 teaspoon vanilla; beat at low speed until blended. Beat at medium speed 2 minutes or until frosting is smooth.

5 Place one cake layer on serving plate; spread with 2 cups frosting. Top with second cake layer; frost top and side of cake with remaining frosting. Press 1¾ cups walnuts onto side of cake. Sprinkle remaining ¼ cup walnuts over top of cake.

CHOCOLATE FROSTY >

MAKES 2 TO 3 SERVINGS

2 cups milk, divided

¼ cup unsweetened cocoa powder

½ cup sweetened condensed milk

1 tablespoon corn syrup

1 teaspoon vanilla

1 Whisk ¼ cup milk and cocoa in large measuring cup with pour spout until well blended. Whisk in 1½ cups milk, sweetened condensed milk, corn syrup and vanilla. Pour mixture into ice cube tray. Freeze 4 hours or until firm.

2 Loosen frozen chocolate cubes with thin knife; remove from ice cube trays. Place in blender with remaining ¼ cup milk; pulse to break up chunks. Blend about 30 seconds or until smooth.

SHAMROCK SHAKE

MAKES 1 SERVING

2 cups low-fat French vanilla ice cream

½ cup milk, divided

⅛ teaspoon peppermint extract

10 drops green food coloring

Whipped cream and maraschino cherry (optional)

Combine ice cream, ¼ cup milk, peppermint extract and green food coloring in blender; blend until smooth, adding additional ¼ cup milk if needed for desired consistency. Pour into glass; garnish with whipped cream and cherry.

TIRAMISU

MAKES 9 SERVINGS

¾ cup sugar

4 egg yolks

1 cup plus 2 tablespoons whipping cream, divided

2 containers (8 ounces each) mascarpone cheese

½ teaspoon vanilla

¾ cup cold strong brewed coffee

¼ cup coffee-flavored liqueur

24 to 28 ladyfingers

2 teaspoons unsweetened cocoa powder

1 Fill medium saucepan half full with water; bring to a boil over high heat. Reduce heat to low to maintain a simmer. Whisk sugar, egg yolks and 2 tablespoons cream in medium metal bowl until well blended. Place bowl over simmering water; cook 6 to 8 minutes or until thickened, whisking constantly. Remove from heat; cool slightly. Whisk in mascarpone and vanilla until smooth and well blended.

2 Pour remaining 1 cup cream into large bowl of electric stand mixer; beat at high speed until stiff peaks form. Gently fold whipped cream into mascarpone mixture until no streaks of white remain.

3 Combine coffee and liqueur in shallow bowl; mix well. Working with one ladyfinger at a time, dip cookies briefly into coffee mixture. Arrange in single layer in 9-inch square baking pan, trimming to fit as necessary. Spread thin layer of custard over ladyfingers, covering completely. Dip remaining ladyfingers in remaining coffee mixture; arrange in single layer over custard. Spread remaining custard over cookies. Place cocoa in fine-mesh strainer; sprinkle over custard. Refrigerate 2 hours or overnight.

LIMONCELLO CAKE WITH MASCARPONE FROSTING

MAKES 8 TO 10 SERVINGS

CAKE

- 2½ cups all-purpose flour
- 1 teaspoon baking powder
- 1 teaspoon baking soda
- ¾ teaspoon salt
- 2 cups granulated sugar
- ¾ cup (1½ sticks) butter, softened
- 4 eggs
- 3 tablespoons grated lemon peel
- ¾ cup buttermilk
- ½ cup lemon juice
- ½ cup plus 1 tablespoon limoncello, divided
- Yellow food coloring (optional)

FROSTING

- 1 cup whipping cream
- ¼ cup powdered sugar
- 1 container (8 ounces) mascarpone cheese
- 2 tablespoons granulated sugar
- 3 tablespoons lemon juice
- White chocolate shavings (optional)

1 For cake, preheat oven to 350°F. Line bottoms of two 9-inch round baking pans with parchment paper; grease and flour pans. Combine flour, baking powder, baking soda and salt in medium bowl; mix well.

2 Beat 2 cups granulated sugar and butter in large bowl with electric mixer at medium-high speed 5 minutes until light and fluffy. Add eggs, one at a time, beating 30 seconds after each addition. Scrape bottom and side of bowl. Add lemon peel; beat at medium-high speed 1 minute.

3 Combine buttermilk and lemon juice in 2-cup measure. With mixer at low speed, alternately add flour mixture, buttermilk mixture and ½ cup limoncello, beginning and ending with flour mixture. Tint batter with food coloring, if desired. Stir with spatula until well blended. Divide batter evenly between prepared pans; smooth top.

4 Bake 25 to 30 minutes or until tops are golden brown and toothpick inserted into centers comes out clean. Cool in pans 10 minutes; remove to wire racks to cool completely.

5 For frosting, beat cream and powdered sugar in large bowl with electric mixer at medium-high speed 2 minutes or until stiff peaks form. Transfer to medium bowl. Combine mascarpone, 2 tablespoons granulated sugar and 3 tablespoons lemon juice in same large bowl. Replace whip with paddle attachment; beat at medium speed 2 minutes or until smooth and well blended. Stir one third of whipped cream into mascarpone mixture. Gently fold in remaining whipped cream until well blended.

6 Place one cake layer on serving plate; brush with half of remaining 1 tablespoon limoncello. Spread half of frosting over cake. Top with second cake layer; brush with remaining limoncello. Spread remaining frosting over top of cake. Garnish with white chocolate shavings.

MARBLED COOKIE BROWNIE

MAKES 9 TO 12 SERVINGS

1 cup plus 1 tablespoon all-purpose flour
½ teaspoon baking soda
½ teaspoon salt
½ cup (1 stick) butter, softened
½ cup packed brown sugar
¼ cup granulated sugar

1 egg
½ teaspoon vanilla extract
1 cup milk chocolate chunks or chips
1 package (18 to 19 ounces) brownie mix, plus ingredients to prepare mix

1 Preheat oven to 350°F. Line 9-inch square baking pan with parchment paper; spray paper with nonstick cooking spray.

2 For cookies, combine flour, baking soda and salt in small bowl; mix well. Beat butter, brown sugar and granulated sugar in large bowl with electric mixer at medium speed about 3 minutes or until light and fluffy, scraping down side of bowl occasionally. Add egg; beat until well blended. Beat in vanilla. Gradually add flour mixture; beat at low speed just until blended. Stir in chocolate chunks. Cover and refrigerate dough while preparing brownies.

3 Prepare brownie mix according to package directions. Spread batter in prepared pan; smooth top. Scoop out eight 1½-tablespoon balls of cookie dough; roll into smooth, round balls. (Reserve remaining cookie dough for another use.) Scatter cookie dough balls over brownie batter; press down gently to push cookie dough into brownie batter.

4 Bake 25 minutes, then cover loosely with foil to prevent cookies from becoming too brown. Bake about 13 minutes or until brownies are firm, edges begin to come away from side of pan and toothpick inserted into center comes out clean. Cool in pan on wire rack 10 minutes. Serve warm or at room temperature.

SNICKERY PIE
MAKES 8 TO 10 SERVINGS

CRUST
- 1½ cups vanilla wafer cookie crumbs
- 3 tablespoons sugar
- 2 tablespoons unsweetened cocoa powder
- ¼ cup (½ stick) butter, melted

FILLING
- 2 cups whipping cream
- 1 package (8 ounces) cream cheese, softened
- ¾ cup dulce de leche
- ¼ cup sugar
- 1 teaspoon vanilla
- 2 chocolate-covered peanut-nougat-caramel candy bars (1.86 ounces each), finely chopped

TOPPING
- ¼ cup dulce de leche
- 3 tablespoons milk
- ½ cup semisweet chocolate chips
- 1½ teaspoons coconut oil
- 2 chocolate-covered peanut-nougat-caramel candy bars (1.86 ounces each), coarsely chopped
- ¼ cup coarsely chopped salted peanuts

1 For crust, preheat oven to 350°F. Combine cookie crumbs, 3 tablespoons sugar and cocoa in medium bowl; mix well. Stir in butter until moistened and well blended. Press mixture onto bottom and up side of 9-inch deep-dish pie plate. Bake 8 minutes. Cool completely on wire rack.

2 For filling, beat 2 cups cream in large bowl with electric mixer at medium-high speed 1 minute or until stiff peaks form. Transfer cream to medium bowl. (Do not wash out mixer bowl.)

3 Combine cream cheese, ¾ cup dulce de leche, ¼ cup sugar and vanilla in same large bowl. Replace whip with paddle attachment; beat at medium speed 1 to 2 minutes or until well blended, scraping bowl and beater once.

4 Gently fold in whipped cream in three additions until well blended (no streaks of white remain). Fold in 2 chopped candy bars. Spread evenly in prepared crust. Refrigerate 4 hours or overnight.

5 For topping, microwave ¼ cup dulce de leche in small bowl on HIGH 20 seconds. Stir; microwave 10 seconds or until softened. Stir in milk until well blended. Combine chocolate and coconut oil in small saucepan; heat over low heat until chocolate is melted and mixture is smooth, stirring frequently. Drizzle dulce de leche and chocolate mixtures over pie; sprinkle with 2 chopped candy bars and peanuts. Refrigerate until topping is set.

BERRY CRUMBLE BARS

MAKES 8 TO 16 SERVINGS

3 cups all-purpose flour

½ cup plus ⅓ cup granulated sugar, divided

½ cup packed brown sugar

1 teaspoon baking powder

1 teaspoon grated lemon peel

½ teaspoon salt

1 cup (2 sticks) cold butter, cut into pieces

1 egg, beaten

2½ tablespoons lemon juice

1 tablespoon cornstarch

1 package (16 ounces) frozen mixed berries (do not thaw)

Vanilla ice cream (optional)

1 Preheat oven to 375°F. Spray 9-inch square baking pan with nonstick cooking spray or line with parchment paper and spray paper with cooking spray.

2 Combine flour, ½ cup granulated sugar, brown sugar, baking powder, lemon peel and salt in large bowl; mix well. Add butter and egg; mix with pastry blender or hands until a crumbly dough forms. Pat one third of dough into prepared pan.

3 Combine remaining ⅓ cup granulated sugar, lemon juice and cornstarch in medium bowl; mix well. Add berries, stir until well blended and berries are completely coated with sugar mixture. Spread evenly over crust. Top with remaining dough, crumbling into large pieces over fruit.

4 Bake 45 to 50 minutes or until top is golden brown. Cool in pan on wire rack. (Refrigerating bars for several hours will make them easier to cut.) Serve with ice cream, if desired.

MOLTEN CHOCOLATE CAKES

MAKES 8 CAKES

1 package (about 15 ounces) chocolate fudge cake mix

1½ cups water

3 eggs

½ cup canola or vegetable oil

4 ounces bittersweet chocolate, chopped

4 ounces semisweet chocolate, chopped

½ cup whipping cream

¼ cup (½ stick) butter, cut into pieces

1 tablespoon light corn syrup

¼ teaspoon vanilla

⅛ teaspoon salt

Caramel ice cream topping

Vanilla ice cream

1 Preheat oven to 350°F. Spray 8 jumbo (3½-inch) muffin cups with nonstick cooking spray.

2 Beat cake mix, water, eggs and oil in large bowl with electric mixer at low speed 30 seconds. Beat at medium speed 2 minutes. Pour ½ cup batter into each prepared muffin cup; discard remaining batter. Bake about 25 minutes or until toothpick inserted into centers comes out clean. Cool in pan 5 minutes; remove to wire racks to cool.

3 Meanwhile, combine bittersweet chocolate, semisweet chocolate, cream, butter, corn syrup, vanilla and salt in medium microwavable bowl; microwave on HIGH 30 seconds. Stir; microwave at additional 30-second intervals until chocolate begins to melt. Whisk until smooth. Reserve ½ cup chocolate mixture in small microwavable bowl for topping.

4 When cakes have cooled, cut off domed top of each cake with serrated knife. Invert cakes so wider part is on the bottom. Use 1½-inch biscuit cutter or small serrated knife to remove hole in top of each cake (narrow part) about 1 inch deep. Reserve cake from holes for serving.

5 Fill hole in each cake with 2 tablespoons chocolate mixture; top with reserved cake pieces. Microwave reserved ½ cup chocolate mixture on HIGH 20 seconds or until melted.

6 For each serving, drizzle caramel topping on microwavable plate. Arrange cake on plate; microwave on HIGH about 30 seconds until chocolate filling is hot. Top with ice cream; drizzle with warm chocolate mixture.

ORANGE WHIP >

MAKES 2 SERVINGS

2 cups ice cubes

1 can (12 ounces) frozen orange juice concentrate with pulp, partially thawed

1 cup milk

¼ cup powdered sugar

½ teaspoon vanilla

Combine ice, orange juice concentrate, milk, powdered sugar and vanilla in blender; pulse to break up ice. Blend until smooth.

COFFEE FRAPPUCCINO

MAKES 1 (16-OUNCE) SERVING

½ cup ground coffee (preferably dark roast)

1 cup water

½ cup milk

¼ cup sweetened condensed milk

2 tablespoons instant vanilla pudding and pie filling mix

1 tablespoon maple syrup

1 cup ice cubes (about 6 cubes)

Whipped cream and unsweetened cocoa powder (optional)

1 Brew strong coffee using ground coffee and water.* (You should get about ½ cup coffee.) Refrigerate until cold.

2 Combine ¼ cup coffee, milk, sweetened condensed milk, pudding mix, maple syrup and ice in blender; blend until smooth. Garnish with whipped cream and cocoa.

This drink requires very strong coffee. If you don't have a coffee maker, you can use 2 tablespoons instant coffee blended with 2 tablespoons hot water or just enough water to dissolve the coffee. Proceed with step 2 as directed.

DESSERTS

CHOCOLATE ECLAIR CAKE

MAKES 12 TO 18 SERVINGS

3¼ cups plus 6 tablespoons whole milk, divided

2 packages (3.4 ounces each) vanilla instant pudding and pie filling mix

1 container (8 ounces) frozen whipped topping, thawed

1⅓ boxes (about 14 ounces each) graham crackers (35 whole graham cracker rectangles)

6 tablespoons (¾ stick) butter

⅓ cup unsweetened dark or regular cocoa powder

Pinch salt

1 teaspoon vanilla extract

2 cups powdered sugar, sifted

1 Whisk 3¼ cups milk and vanilla pudding mixes in large bowl about 2 minutes. Fold in whipped topping until well blended.

2 Cover bottom of 13×9-inch pan with single layer of graham crackers, cutting to fit as needed. Pour one third of pudding mixture (about 2½ cups) over graham crackers; smooth top with spatula. Repeat layers twice. Top with remaining graham crackers, arranging them bumpy side down over pudding mixture.

3 Combine remaining 6 tablespoons milk and butter in large microwavable bowl; microwave on HIGH 30 seconds. Stir; microwave 30 seconds or until butter is melted. Add cocoa and salt; whisk until blended. Stir in vanilla. Add powdered sugar; whisk until well blended and smooth.

4 Pour chocolate icing over graham crackers, spreading in even layer and covering top completely. Refrigerate 8 hours or overnight.

RESTAURANT INDEX

RECIPE INDEX

TRADEMARKS

Another Broken Egg Cafe is a registered trademark of Another Broken Egg of America Franchising LLC.

Applebee's is a registered trademark of Applebee's Restaurants LLC.

Au Bon Pain is a registered trademark of ABP CORPORATION.

Auntie Anne's is a registered trademark of Auntie Anne's Franchisor SPV LLC.

Baker's Square is a registered trademark of American Blue Ribbon Holdings, LLC.

Benihana is a registered trademark of Benihana National Corp.

Bertucci's is a registered trademark of Bertucci's Corporation.

BJ's Restaurant & Brewhouse is a registered trademark of BJ's Restaurants, Inc.

Boston Market is a registered trademark of Boston Market Corporation.

Buffalo Wild Wings is a registered trademark of Buffalo Wild Wings, Inc.

Burger King is a registered trademark of Burger King Corporation.

California Pizza Kitchen is a registered trademark of California Pizza Kitchen, Inc.

Carrabba's Italian Grill is a registered trademark of Bloomin' Brands, Inc.

The Cheesecake Factory is a registered trademark of TFC Co. LLC.

Chili's is a registered trademark of Brinker International.

Chipotle Mexican Grill is a registered trademark of Chipotle Mexican Grill.

Cinnabon is a registered trademark of Cinnabon® Franchisor SPV LLC.

Cracker Barrel is a registered trademark of CBOCS Properties, Inc.

Domino's Pizza is a registered trademark of Domino's IP Holder LLC.

Earls is a registered trademark of Earls Restaurants Ltd.

El Pollo Loco is a registered trademark of El Pollo Loco.

Fazoli's is a registered trademark of Fazoli's System Management, LLC.

First Watch is a registered trademark of First Watch Restaurants, Inc.

Hooter's is a registered trademark of Hooters of America, LLC.

Huddle House is a registered trademark of Huddle House, Inc.

IHOP is a registered trademark of IHOP Restaurants LLC.

Jason's Deli is a registered trademark of Deli Management, Inc.

Johnny Carino's is a registered trademark of Fired Up Inc.

KFC is a registered trademark of Yum! Brands, Inc.

Lone Star Steakhouse is a registered trademark of LSF5 CACTUS, LLC.

Longhorn Steakhouse is a registered trademark of Darden Concepts, Inc.

Maggiano's Little Italy is a registered trademark of Maggiano's Little Italy.

Margaritaville is a registered trademark of MARGARITAVILLE.

Marie Callender's is a registered trademark of Perkins & Marie Callender's®, LLC.

McDonald's is a registered trademark of McDonald's.

Mimi's Cafe is a registered trademark of SWH MIMI'S CAFE, LLC.

Morton's The Steakhouse is a registered trademark of Landry's, Inc.

Olive Garden is a registered trademark of Darden Concepts, Inc.

Orange Julius is a registered trademark of American Dairy Queen Corp.

Outback Steakhouse is a registered trademark of Bloomin' Brands, Inc.

Panera Bread is a registered trademark of Panera Bread.

Pei Wei is a registered trademark of Pei Wei Asian Diner, LLC.

P.F. Chang's is a registered trademark of P.F. Chang's China Bistro, Inc.

Portillo's is a registered trademark of Portillo's.

Red Lobster is a registered trademark of Red Lobster Hospitality, LLC.

Red Robin is a registered trademark of Red Robin International, Inc.

Ruth's Chris is a registered trademark of Ruth's Hospitality Group.

Snooze is a registered trademark of Snooze.

Starbucks is a registered trademark of Starbucks Coffee Company.

Sweet Tomatoes is a registered trademark of Sweet Tomatoes.

Taco Bell is a registered trademark of Taco Bell IP Holder, LLC.

TGI Fridays is a registered trademark of TGI Fridays, Inc.

Tropical Smoothie Cafe is a registered trademark of Tropical Smoothie Cafe, LLC.

Wendy's is a registered trademark of Wendy's International, LLC.

METRIC CONVERSION CHART

VOLUME MEASUREMENTS (dry)

1/8 teaspoon = 0.5 mL
1/4 teaspoon = 1 mL
1/2 teaspoon = 2 mL
3/4 teaspoon = 4 mL
1 teaspoon = 5 mL
1 tablespoon = 15 mL
2 tablespoons = 30 mL
1/4 cup = 60 mL
1/3 cup = 75 mL
1/2 cup = 125 mL
2/3 cup = 150 mL
3/4 cup = 175 mL
1 cup = 250 mL
2 cups = 1 pint = 500 mL
3 cups = 750 mL
4 cups = 1 quart = 1 L

VOLUME MEASUREMENTS (fluid)

1 fluid ounce (2 tablespoons) = 30 mL
4 fluid ounces (1/2 cup) = 125 mL
8 fluid ounces (1 cup) = 250 mL
12 fluid ounces (1 1/2 cups) = 375 mL
16 fluid ounces (2 cups) = 500 mL

WEIGHTS (mass)

1/2 ounce = 15 g
1 ounce = 30 g
3 ounces = 90 g
4 ounces = 120 g
8 ounces = 225 g
10 ounces = 285 g
12 ounces = 360 g
16 ounces = 1 pound = 450 g

DIMENSIONS

1/16 inch = 2 mm
1/8 inch = 3 mm
1/4 inch = 6 mm
1/2 inch = 1.5 cm
3/4 inch = 2 cm
1 inch = 2.5 cm

OVEN TEMPERATURES

250°F = 120°C
275°F = 140°C
300°F = 150°C
325°F = 160°C
350°F = 180°C
375°F = 190°C
400°F = 200°C
425°F = 220°C
450°F = 230°C

BAKING PAN SIZES

Utensil	Size in Inches/Quarts	Metric Volume	Size in Centimeters
Baking or Cake Pan (square or rectangular)	8×8×2	2 L	20×20×5
	9×9×2	2.5 L	23×23×5
	12×8×2	3 L	30×20×5
	13×9×2	3.5 L	33×23×5
Loaf Pan	8×4×3	1.5 L	20×10×7
	9×5×3	2 L	23×13×7
Round Layer Cake Pan	8×1½	1.2 L	20×4
	9×1½	1.5 L	23×4
Pie Plate	8×1¼	750 mL	20×3
	9×1¼	1 L	23×3
Baking Dish or Casserole	1 quart	1 L	—
	1½ quart	1.5 L	—
	2 quart	2 L	—